Fiona McIntosh-Varjabédian, Alison Boulanger (eds.)

Comparing Literatures:
Aspects, Method, and Orientation

Proceedings of the 8th Congress of the
European Society of Comparative Literature (ESCL-SELC)

Fiona McIntosh-Varjabédian, Alison Boulanger (eds.)

COMPARING LITERATURES: ASPECTS, METHOD, AND ORIENTATION

Proceedings of the 8th Congress of the
European Society of Comparative Literature (ESCL-SELC)

Bibliografische Information der Deutschen Nationalbibliothek
Die Deutsche Nationalbibliothek verzeichnet diese Publikation in der Deutschen Nationalbibliografie; detaillierte bibliografische Daten sind im Internet über http://dnb.d-nb.de abrufbar.

Bibliographic information published by the Deutsche Nationalbibliothek
Die Deutsche Nationalbibliothek lists this publication in the Deutsche Nationalbibliografie; detailed bibliographic data are available in the Internet at http://dnb.d-nb.de.

ISBN-13: 978-3-8382-1428-3
© *ibidem*-Verlag, Stuttgart 2022
Alle Rechte vorbehalten

Das Werk einschließlich aller seiner Teile ist urheberrechtlich geschützt. Jede Verwertung außerhalb der engen Grenzen des Urheberrechtsgesetzes ist ohne Zustimmung des Verlages unzulässig und strafbar. Dies gilt insbesondere für Vervielfältigungen, Übersetzungen, Mikroverfilmungen und elektronische Speicherformen sowie die Einspeicherung und Verarbeitung in elektronischen Systemen.

All rights reserved. No part of this publication may be reproduced, stored in or introduced into a retrieval system, or transmitted, in any form, or by any means (electronical, mechanical, photocopying, recording or otherwise) without the prior written permission of the publisher. Any person who does any unauthorized act in relation to this publication may be liable to criminal prosecution and civil claims for damages.

Printed in the EU

Table of Contents

Fiona McIntosh-Varjabédian
Introduction. Comparative Literature-World Literature: Spreading Knowledge and Representations between Cultural Curiosity and the Risk of New Globish Stereotypes 7

Part 1. Translation as Mediation between Languages and Literatures 19

Lieven D'hulst
How Translation Knowledges Travel in Space and Time 21

Joseph Pivato
Comparative Literature: A Revitalization 43

Part 2. Making a Difference in Language, Literature and Literary Theory 59

Alison Boulanger
Nabokov's Languages 61

Tamar Barbakadze
Proust's and Woolf's Dialogue Regarding Language 75

Olga Szmidt
The Discreet Charm of Refraining from Judgment. A Few Doubts Concerning Evaluation in Contemporary Literary Criticism 89

Part 3. Mediating between Images and Wor(l)ds 109

Sandro Jung
The Transnational Reach and Interpretation-Shaping Power of Book Illustrations and Defoe's *Robinson Crusoe* in 1720 111

Jobst Welge
The Transmission of Knowledge in European Adventure Fiction of the Amazon 135

Orsolya Milián
The Blind Leading the Blind: Brueghel in Ekphrastic Poetry 149

Introduction.
Comparative Literature-World Literature: Spreading Knowledge and Representations between Cultural Curiosity and the Risk of New Globish Stereotypes

Fiona McIntosh-Varjabédian (Université de Lille)

From one conference to another, the same doubts and laments seem to re-emerge.[1] The legitimacy of comparative literature is questioned for often opposite reasons: is it too centred on a very limited cultural area, *i.e.* mainly European? or does it tend to be too globish when it expands its views to world literature? For a bi-annual conference of the European Society of Comparative Literature, the question seems even more acute, since most contributors came from European countries and many worked on languages and literatures from the European area.

As often, oppositions are not as clear-cut as they may seem in the first place. While Emily Apter criticizes some institutional forms of World Literature studies and "harbour[s] serious reservations about tendencies in World Literature toward reflexive endorsement of cultural equivalence and substitutability," considering that many celebrations "of nationally and ethnically branded 'differences' [...] have been niche-marketed as commercialized 'identities,'" she definitely sides with one of the main assumptions of World Literature studies, *i.e.* the necessary "deprovincialization of the canon" (Apter: 2). A great promoter of these studies at Yale, David Damrosch echoes Apter's reservations and underlines the risk of "reducing [a foreign text] to a pallid version of some literary form we already know" when its foreignness is not properly taken into account" (Damrosch: 1). He reminds his reader of the possible shortcomings of cultural transfers. For, as he admits, giving a new

---

[1] See, for instance, Tomiche or Du.

life to a literary text in a new language and in a new culture "can involve both losses and gains" (Damrosch: 1). However, despite the awareness Damrosch shares with Pascale Casanova that cultural transfers can be unequal and might be dictated by the laws of commerce and by imperial cultural domination, whatever form it may take (Casanova, 2008; Casanova, 2015), he makes a leap of faith, driven by the "conviction that works of world literature have an exceptional ability to transcend the boundaries of cultures that produced them" (Damrosch: 2). The humanistic assumptions that lie behind this conviction are obvious, indicating that between the cultural networks of the past so-called "republic of letters" and the new networks of this global era, there is a continuum.

Though some great works may seem untranslatable because their meaning is linked to a given time and a given place, others can be meaningful beyond a "homegrown audience" and can find "a compelling immediacy" that paradoxically can go with a sense of "persisting foreignness" (Damrosch: 3). What if the role of comparative literature was precisely to conciliate both the impressions of immediacy and of foreignness described by Damrosch and to make the reader aware of the limitations of both? Should we not embrace the so-called limitations of our discipline at last and consider them less as insufferable flaws than as a productive and stimulating caveat? To take pains to understand a specific culture, the possibilities offered by its language, and the implicit assumptions and hierarchies at the heart of its own culture is certainly a necessary step to promote real understanding and overcome the dangers of globishness. At the same time, if we wish indeed to consider literature as a "fund of cultural knowledge" (Damrosch: 1) that is valuable and illuminating, beyond space and time, cultural transfers and translations–for all their necessary limitations and even their misinterpretations–play a crucial role in ensuring cultural dialogue, even if it can be at the price of a certain dose of loss and even of frustration.

The period during which Goethe coined the successful expression of *Weltliteratur* is useful to understand both the ideals and the pitfalls at the heart of the subject. Nothing is entirely new under the sun and many of our contemporary debates on subaltern literatures echo the strategies and the doubts of the German writers at the end of the 18th Century, with the exportation and dissemination of the Herderian formula in Europe: against the cultural imperialism of a dominant language and literature, French at the time, the differentiation of small literatures was achieved by finding new resources in oral culture and by equating national literature, national culture and national language. The ennobling process of collecting ballads and tales as popular forms of epics was adopted not only by other European writers during the century to give legitimacy to their political claims, it was exported and adopted a century later by other nascent countries during the decolonisation, as Pascale Casanova underlines (Casanova 2008: 321-324).

But are not these forms of differentiation and revolt against dominant cultures partly illusionary, as they answer global demands for niche products? Germaine de Stael's assertion at the beginning of *Corinne ou l'Italie* (Chapter IV) can indeed be understood both ways:

> The art of civilization tends continuously to make all the men similar in appearance and almost in reality; but the spirit and the imagination take pleasure in the differences which characterize the nations: men resemble each other only by affectation or by calculation; but all that is natural is varied.[2]

In the opposition the writer draws between civilized uniformity and natural variety, the balance seems at first to tip on the side of the latter, through the many pleasures that nature offers over the implicit boredom provided by unified cosmopolitanism and civilization. "Affectation" and "calculation" denote artificialness and search for profit and appear as mildly derogatory. But of which nature is this pleasure exactly? In a novel which represents on the one hand the Grand Tour of a melancholic member of the British

---

[2] All translations are mine unless otherwise indicated. "L'art de la civilisation tend sans cesse à rendre tous les hommes semblables en apparence et presque en réalité; mais l'esprit et l'imagination se plaisent dans les différences qui caractérisent les nations: les hommes ne se ressemblent entre eux que par l'affectation ou le calcul; mais tout ce qui est naturel est varié." Germaine de Staël, *Corinne ou l'Italie*, book I, chap. IV: 39.

Elite and on the other the patriotic and lyrical flights of a female Poet Laureate, the answer may seem grimmer. By the rejection of Corinne by Oswald's father and by Oswald himself, the young woman who symbolises Italy and its poetical voice can only seem to offer a colourful but momentary entertainment. The vocabulary of the picturesque and of the sublime associates the intense admiration for Italian culture with decay, because the Peninsula, as Corinne sings, is no longer at the heart of the European world. Its admirable originality is linked in the novel to its marginality and its subalternity is symbolized by the heroine who is supposed to give voice to Italy itself, before sinking into despair and dying.

Fortunately, there are far happier experiences of literary diversity and of cultural rebellions against a dominant culture, but the danger of mere picturesqueness or of mere exotism remains. However, Goethe's own poetic and literary enterprise, as described by F. Strich, may offer an answer to the conundrum (Strich: 19-27). It is well known that Schiller and Goethe abandoned the Herderian ideals of the *Sturm und Drang*, and reverted to a kind of new Classicism that meant a breach with the exclusiveness of national inspiration. After having reappropriated and discussed Shakespeare's legacy in *Wilhelm Meisters Lehrjahre*, 1795, adapted and translated Voltaire in 1802, Goethe found inspiration outside Europe in Hafez, in the *West-östlicher Divan* (1819). As Strich demonstrates, there is no stringent opposition between national literature and world literature for Goethe, as he overcomes the divide by discovering the universal in national poetry and contexts and, conversely, by finding sources of originality and singularity in the many manifestations of the universal itself. Encounters with other literatures are inspiring, both by referring to the contexts in which they were born, as Goethe did in his notes and introduction to the *West-östlicher Divan*, and by reappropriating and recontextualising these works, in a sense that they can convey a new meaning outside what the authors intended in the first place, as he did in the poems themselves.

Can Goethe's legacy provide us with a method? To which extent is it necessary to plunge into the mindset, the mores and the language of a given context? According to a philological approach to literature, the context is considered traditionally as a means "to elucidate the total import of the text which is the primary cause and ultimate target of literary scholarship as well as the chief instrument of its verification" (Remak: 247). However, if the proof lies primarily in the text and its context, we must also ask ourselves to which extent it is allowable to recontextualize a work and adapt its reading and message to another culture. The issue has been amply discussed when unequal intercultural relations have given birth to acculturation and cultural appropriation. These can be defined when "a relatively more powerful group was in sustained contact with a less powerful one" (Jackson: 86) or when "majorities attempt to reshape minorities in their image," (Jackson: 87) and "aspects of the culture of the subordinated group, making them [their] own" (Jackson: 88). In these cases, re-contextualisation erases "the complex, networked nature of social life" (Jackson: 105) and petrifies living practices into fake traditions. The uproar concerning the translation of Amanda Gorman's poems into Dutch or Catalan demonstrates how political the recontextualization of a literary work can be. Although the poetess herself did not challenge Marieke Lucas Rijneveld's right to translate her work, the translation by an author of an altogether different background and identity was seen by some as a betrayal of the poetess's moving experience of subalternity.

The problems we are facing are not only linked to the act of translating and adapting contemporary works and texts between two cultures of unequal power or prestige. A similar problem arises when dealing with the literary canon itself: each retranslation begs the question whether a masterpiece of the past should be adapted or not to the present times. The debates are still rife as prove the disagreements between, on the one hand, Danièle Robert in France who wished to respect the *Terza rima* of the Divine Comedy, and its complex and multi-layered language, as far as it was possible, and on the other, Lies Lavrijsen who, in a Dutch translation, decided to simplify the poet's style and adapt it to a new young public while expunging historical allusions that seemed possibly offensive to the translator.

These recent disputes point out the many ambiguities of translation itself, as it can be defined, according to the Merriam Webster dictionary, not only as turning "into one's own or another language" but as transferring "from one set of symbols into another." So it can be understood both as the capacity to express the same ideas "in different terms and especially different words" and thus to paraphrase. It can be seen as an explanation or an interpretation, and even as a transfer or a transformation. Each definition shows how it can be removed from the original and even replace it when the words and the references become too obscure to be understood spontaneously by a non-scholarly by a non-scholarly or a foreign audience.

Among the difficulties that are due to specific contexts, the understanding of the knowledge embedded in literary texts is one of the hardest to address. Christine Baron defines the term *savoir* that cannot strictly be equated with science:

> What we call knowing (savoir) is the way in which knowledge (*connaissances*) takes shape. This knowledge has a scientific basis but it also has marked social and cultural characteristics. These characteristics are the object of public debate which in short, in its principles, its dissemination, its application, concerns forms of living together. It is in this sense that the word "knowledge" can be understood in its articulation with literary texts.[3]

Baron follows Pierre Macherey and his conviction that poems and novels are not read for the cognitive knowledge they may contain. Fiction and poetry as such may seem out of the boundaries of science, although the divide was certainly less of strong before the 19th Century: even the erotic novel *Les Bijoux indiscrets* (1748) came to represent the debates between Cartesians and Newtonians, announcing some of Diderot's considerations in his *Principes philosophiques de la matière et du mouvement* (1770, published in

---

[3] "Ce qu'on appelle savoir est la manière dont prennent corps des connaissances qui ont un socle scientifique mais qui ont également des caractéristiques sociales et culturelles marquées, qui sont objet de débats publics, bref qui concernent dans leurs principes, leur diffusion, leur application, des formes du vivre ensemble. C'est en ce sens que le mot 'savoir' peut être compris dans son articulation avec les textes littéraires," Baron: 51-52.

1792).[4] In their very representations however, writers are indebted to paradigms (Séginger, 69-79) and to the intellectual networks to which they belong. These networks disseminate the scientific ideas or build the common references of a well-informed intellectual, and as such they belong to the realm of comparative literature. But not to mention the question of influences, Foucault demonstrated in *Les Mots et les Choses* that images are not mere ornaments, they may refer to strong beliefs before they become hackneyed and lose their evocative power; up to the end of the 16th Century resemblances themselves were considered as tokens of an existing link between plants and beings inside the terrestrial microcosm, or as means to re-establish the correspondence between the macrocosm of celestial order and the mutability of the sublunary world (Foucault: 33-59). Similes and metaphors make sense inside a given paradigm: amongst the European atheists Man was represented as a machine until the mechanist model was eventually replaced by a biological one.

We ourselves are witnessing a change of paradigm in the contemporary literature we are reading and studying. Our research itself is affected by the ongoing practical reorganization of our institutions and the changing expectations these institutions have concerning the meaning and the uses of knowledge and culture. Such changes also have had epistemological consequences of which we could only give a glimpse, during the 8th Conference of the European Society of Comparative Literature that took place in Lille (26-30th August, 2019).

We asked ourselves how the status of literature, the processes by which it is created, produced, disseminated, had been modified, whether the way in which literature takes its place within society had changed, and if so, in what way. We also examined, as seen above, the effect of economic globalization over cultural globalization: does the birth of a "world literature" mean that literary creation is becoming uniform, or on the contrary does it arouse an antagonistic tendency towards expressing and highlighting local and regional cultures? We asked what

---

[4] See Wolfe: 312; Aram: 377.

globalization meant for cultural exchanges. How is the relation to the other, to the foreigner built, at such a juncture? In this light, it was useful to gain perspective by relating such questions to more ancient periods which were noted for their openness to the world, and their willingness to accept new paradigms, such as the Renaissance, birth-period of the "Gutenberg galaxy," a time when widescale maritime explorations, with attendant cultural discoveries and cultural antagonisms, sowed the seeds of a still-ongoing debate about hierarchized and de-hierarchized, centralized and de-centralized exchanges. In ancient no less than in recent times, the development of new technological possibilities has had a radical impact on the questions which are debated within the humanities.

Of all the papers delivered in the course of this Congress, we offer the following sample in the hope that it will aptly reflect the issues under debate. Thus, in the first section, where Lieven D'hulst considers how to map translation and translation history, and Joseph Pivato compares the importance of foreign languages in literature studies throughout American and Canadian academia, both researchers make a case for the vitality of plurilingual exchanges, at a time when they are under threat from the hegemony of one main language. As Lieven D'hulst writes in conclusion, "At a moment when global science threatens diversity in thinking, historians of knowledge may very well be the true guardians of the interconnected diversity across the world" (D'hulst: 32).

The next section, where the question of translation plays a much less conspicuous part, is a no less passionate plea against uniformity and the indifference it fosters, whether it takes the form of an illusory, surface unity in the English language (as shown in Boulanger's paper on Nabokov's *Pale Fire*), of ubiquitous and supposedly universal set-phrases in propaganda (denounced by Proust and Woolf, as Barbakadze shows in her paper), or of an unruffled, bland critical consensus (which Szmidt's paper takes issue with). While indifference is a very real threat to language, literature and literary criticism, all three can find new vigour in resisting uniformity. Thus Nabokov's protagonists function as unquiet spirits, calling attention to unexpected and fertile differences; Proust and Woolf, lone wolves, resist the urge to howl with the pack, undermining the consensus of their time. Such authors have counterparts in the world of literary criticism, as shown by Szmidt who (along with other critics) pleads for vigorous debate, even if it results in quarrelling over differences. Rather than seek convergence and resemblance, which can result in shallowness, and in a complete inability to conceptualize difference of any kind, authors, readers and critics alike should be on the alert for difference. This tenet will not appear particularly revolutionary to fellow comparatists, as comparative literature tends to establish convergence only to further a relish for divergence — to quote Nabokov's fictitious poet and professor of literature John Shade, "Resemblances are the shadows of differences" (Nabokov, note to line 894: 208).

The fruitfulness of difference, in the final section, is taken up by three articles devoted to the relationship (or rather rivalry) between verbal and visual representation. Sandro Jung examines successive editions of *Robinson Crusoe* in its original English, as well as in French-, Dutch- and German-speaking editions, focusing on the illustrations which were chosen (and, sometimes, specifically commissioned) for those editions, inasmuch as they played an instrumental part in framing and directing interpretation of the tale. Where the original London edition suggested a thrilling tale of adventures in the wild, successive Continental editions firmly established *Robinson Crusoe* as a narrative of religious conversion and repentance — a reading which imbued the wilderness, and the civilizing efforts of the shipwrecked Robinson, with moral implications. A similar overlay of anthropocentric and ethical implications is to be found within the lush descriptions of nature that abound in two novels by Jules Verne and Arthur Conan Doyle, examined by Jobst Welge in the next article. In both Jung's and Welge's articles, the power-struggle between nature and culture is mirrored by a twin conflict between image and text — an issue which becomes even more central in the ultimate article of this volume, when Orsolya Milian examines the shifting relationship between painting and verbal interpretation or re-creation, in this case between Brueghel's *The Blind Leading the Blind*, which has inspired many conflicting interpretations (and sometimes baffled all efforts at interpreting), and two of the ekphrases it gave birth to.

All these papers, in other words, harp on a power struggle, whether it is the struggle of difference against a hegemonic current or the struggle of a reputedly inferior art-form against the discourse that frames its interpretation. Say not the struggle naught availeth, however, since the successive articles in this volume show, on the contrary, how lively and fruitful this vital fight can become.

References

Primary Sources

Staël, Germaine de. *Corinne ou l'Italie* [1807]. Paris: Gallimard [coll. Folio classiques], 1985.

Nabokov, Vladimir. *Pale Fire* [1962]. London: Penguin Books, 1973.

Critical References

Apter, Emily. *Against World-Literature — On the Politics of Untranslatability*. London, New York: Verso, 2013.

Baron, Christine. "Ce que savoir en littérature veut dire." In Anne Tomiche, ed., *Le Comparatisme comme approche critique, Littérature, science, savoirs et technologie*, 6 volumes. Paris: Classiques Garnier, 2017, vol. 6: 51-68.

Casanova, Pascale. *La République mondiale des lettres* [1999]. Paris: Seuil, 2008.

Casanova, Pascale. *La Langue mondiale, traduction et domination*. Paris: Seuil, 2015.

Damrosch, David. *How to Read World Literature*. Newark, Oxford: Wiley Blackwell, 2018 (2nd edition).

D'hulst, Lieven. "How Translation Knowledges Travel in Space and Time." In Fiona McIntosh-Varjabédian and Alison Boulanger (eds.), *Comparing Literatures: Aspects, Method and Orientation*. Stuttgart: Ibidem, 2022: 15-37.

Du, Ping. "Another Argument on the 'Crisis Said' of Comparative Literature." *CLCWeb: Comparative Literature and Culture* 19/5 (2017), *Special Issue Against the "Death" of the Discipline of Comparative Literature*, Shunqing Cao (ed.), 2: http://docs.lib.purdue.edu/clcweb/vol19/iss5/4

Foucault, Michel. *Les Mots et les Choses, Une archéologie des sciences humaines*. Paris: Gallimard, [1966], 1990.

Jackson, J. B. "On Cultural Appropriation." *Journal of Folklore Research*, 58/1 (2021): 77-122. Doi: http://dx.doi.org.ressources-electroniques.univ-lille.fr/10.2979/jfolkrese.58.1.04.

Remak, Henry. "Origins and Evolution of Comparative Literature and its Interdisciplinary Studies." *Heliocon*, 29 (2002/09): 245-250.

Séginger, Gisèle. "Littérature et science, La notion de paradigm." In A. Tomiche, ed., *Le Comparatisme comme approche critique, op. cit.*, vol. 6: 69-79.

Strich, Fritz. *Goethe und die Weltliteratur*. Bern: Francke Verlag, Zweite, verbesserte und ergänzte Auflage, 1957.

Tomiche, Anne. "Comparatism as a Critical Approach." In A. Tomiche, ed., *Le Comparatisme comme approche critique, op. cit.*, vol. 6: 18-30.

Vartanian, Aram. "Erotisme et philosophie chez Diderot." *Cahiers de l'Association internationale des études francaises*, 13 (1961): 367-390. DOI: https://doi.org/10.3406/caief.1961.2210.

Wolf, Charles. *La Philosophie de la biologie avant la biologie, Une histoire du vitalisme*. Paris: Garnier, 2019.

Part 1.
Translation as Mediation between Languages and Literatures

Part I.

How Translation Knowledges Travel in Space and Time[1]

Lieven D'hulst (KU Leuven)

1. Some challenges of translation history

The history of translation interweaves with the history of most practices that make an extensive use of language, such as literature, religion, education, philosophy, law, business, politics, as well as many sciences. All embody more or less specific views on translation and what they expect it to achieve in their realm: to learn languages, spread ideas, sustain trade, exercise rights, impose rules, remodel genres, convert people, and so on.[2] Moreover, as translation unfolds worldwide over extensive periods, it has received countless names: from Latin *vertere* to Chinese *fanyi*, Arabo-Persian *tarjama*, Finnish *kääntää*, or Polish *przekład*, with meanings stretching from the rendering of words to the conveying of entire cultures. Being an act of interlingual communication, translation is further embedded in networks of communicating instances or agents: translators in the first place, but also authorities encouraging (or deterring) translations, publishers selecting and repackaging books to be translated as well as marketing the distribution of translations, educators teaching translation techniques and norms, activists of all sorts using or manipulating translations for propaganda aims, readers buying and commenting on translations.

The long and complex history of translation and translational communication is the subject matter of translation histories. Yet, however fascinating the past may be in its own right, the historian's interest in it is to a large extent rooted in present concerns. In

---

[1] A slightly adapted version of this contribution has been issued in French (D'hulst, 2022).
[2] See Delisle and Woodsworth (2012) for a brief but comprehensive overview of such historical functions.

addition to the myriad of personal reasons that may direct historians, often unintentionally, towards specific facts, figures, periods, or areas, there are more general spheres of interest, or driving forces, shared by larger groups of historians. Today, one of these is that all citizens should have unlimited access to texts, ideas, values, or knowledges of all sorts, across language communities and geopolitical entities. Another one is that bridges should be built when intercultural dialogue fades and when societies tend to close their borders to other worldviews.

Translation history is a demanding undertaking, as it supposes knowledge about the many practices that make use of translation and as it must seek suitable means to account for the array of translational functions, meanings and networks. Obviously, historians may rely on existing research traditions and acquired expertise, but they will also look for innovative or more adequate tools, as made available by other disciplines, including those whose practices they are investigating.[3] However, borrowing as such is not always an option, simply because tools that were tailored for specific objects do not easily adapt to other ones, i.e. translations. In many cases, translation historians need to be imaginative, find alternative ways to deal with the subject at stake, or decide to focus on other subjects.

Take the well-known matter of gathering and mapping data, e.g. translations, translators, genres, techniques, source and target languages, etc. Retrospective sources like library catalogues or national bibliographies are often incomplete or difficult to align, which makes the elaboration and handling of extensive datasets, including longer periods and several languages, a hazardous undertaking. Even more, when it comes to gathering and mapping data relating to past critics, teachers and scholars, or handbooks, essays, and treaties, the typical sources are of little use. Catalogues and libraries rarely use 'translation' as a keyword, while much of the information on translation is to be found in journal articles,

---

[3] Recent translation history offers numerous cases, such as an approach of translated poetry through distant reading techniques (Blakesley, 2016), or a study of French translations of Darwin making use of lexicometric tools (Vandaele, 2019).

essays and reviews that are rarely fully searchable in digitalized form. Obviously, unpublished material, like private correspondences, or working notes, and know-how transmitted orally between e.g. teachers and students, are quite hard if not impossible to access. And so, historians spending a lot of time in libraries and archives nevertheless face the risk of providing partial, speculative or biased reconstructions of past (views on) translations.

By contrast, the digital tools at the disposal of historians who focus on contemporary translations and other aspects of translational communication, such as translation theories or researchers, seem to offer a much firmer grip. For instance, statistical research applied to language use in the scholarly domain has been able to establish that contemporary translation studies has witnessed over the past few decades a growing use of English in publications, preceding even all other languages taken together during the period 2000-2015 (Dong and Chen, 2015). But it has also revealed topic-bound distributions of more languages.[4] All the same, bibliometric studies (a.o. Franco Aixelà, 2013; Agost, 2015; Rovira et al., 2019) based on databases (cf. Bitra; Franco Aixelà, 2001-2018) have opened and explored an array of research avenues, such as citation analysis, keyword analysis, distinction between types of publication (books, articles, conference proceedings), frequency of research areas and topics, and impact of journals, publishing houses, publications and so-called key opinion leaders. The overall picture of translation studies resulting from such combined statistical data is that of a dynamic scientific field, with numerous subdomains, trends and evolutionary lines.

More is undoubtedly needed to address the complex mechanisms that regulate language uses in the social and human sciences, as well as scholarly exchanges across national and continental areas or the growing internationalisation of Anglo-American universities and their research infrastructures. As both

---

[4] For instance, Agost pointed out that "English is the preferred language for some topics of research: theory (53.4%), profession (57%), and audiovisual (55.4%). Conversely, in the area of terminology, English accounts for only 30% of the total" (Agost, 2015: 256).

book-history and field-oriented translation sociology have argued, these mechanisms depend on far-reaching economic and political power relations (Heilbron et al., 2018), which have an enduring impact on the circulation of translation studies as well. One may therefore hope that a conjunction of sociological and bibliometric approaches will further the reconstruction of exchange processes during their most recent history.

As said, and in spite of the fast growth of digital humanities, translation historians working on earlier periods, notably those prior to the 20th century, cannot rely today on comparable rich datasets. As a consequence, statements on the circulation of translations and especially theories and alike will not be systematically underpinned by bibliometrics, or the latter will apply to smaller corpora.[5] Additional, or alternative, ways to handle the same subject resort to other approaches, such as hermeneutics or micro-history, which may foreground no less indispensable features. For instance, the analysis of transfer modalities (excerpting, paraphrasing, summarizing, censoring, etc., cf. M. Götz, 2019) extends beyond the frequency count of specific keywords but is a condition for laying bare and interpreting structural or value changes made to the texts that move from one intellectual domain to another. All the same, micro-history may reveal cases of non-transfer due to less conspicuous reasons such as troublesome relations between scholars, lack of financial resources, or poor marketing by publishers.

Still, one may question the rationale behind the efforts to look for such additional or alternative ways. If power relations seem to steer today the circulation of translations and translation theories, is there a reason to assume that things turned out differently in the

---

[5] The potential of digital humanities for translation history seems to be equally significant in the domain of text analysis. As Wakabayashi argues, the study of "a corpus-informed approach (e.g. concordancing; retrieving lexical clusters) can be applied to certain aspects of translation history, such as analysing translated works or paratexts, oral history transcripts […]. Pinpointing conceptual clusters could be particularly useful, for instance, in examining historical texts discussing translation theory. Automated semantic analysis can identify classes of comments in paratexts, revealing patterns in how translators have conceptualized the act of translating" (Wakabayashi, 2019b: 136-137).

past (with other languages, e.g. Latin, Arabic, or French)? Conversely, what could be the benefit of studying modes of circulation that involve smaller cultures and less-spread languages, during so many periods and in so many places? The answer has become self-evident today. A more variegated and refined investigation of the circulation of translations and ideas on translation should help to correct a number of clichés that are deep-seated in the cultural memories of human societies: about the nature of translation, its forms, functions, ideologies, policies, agents or effects. If this answer applies to the present, it will also apply to the study of past translations and past views on translation.

The task of translation history consists of finding and implementing adequate avenues into past translation and knowledges on translation. This contribution will pay particular attention to the subject of knowledge, and more precisely the historical dissemination of translation knowledge within and especially beyond national, areal, or language borders. The following paragraph takes a closer look at the main concepts at stake, the next one offers a state of the art of knowledge history, the last one suggests some opportunities for further study (including a small toolset that should underpin the promotion of historical research in this domain).

2. On knowledge exchange

Knowledge (*Wissen, savoir*) is one of the buzzwords of contemporary public discourse. It "touches upon almost all spheres of life in all eras and in all regions of the world [...]" (Lässig, 2016: 32). We live in a "knowledge society," in which "knowledge exchange" is an indispensable way to handle complex social questions in relation with climate, economy, education, urbanism, health and other major domains. As we know, universities' so-called stakeholders, as well as larger professional and social communities, seek more intensively than before to cooperate with academic researchers in order to find breeding ground for a wide range of creative insights, which seem beneficial to all partners involved. Numerous projects that make it their central goal to share knowledge are burgeoning worldwide, in many shapes and pursuing countless aims. One example is the "knowledge exchange" project recently launched by the "Oxford Research Centre in the Humanities" (2013):[6]

> Whether working with a theatre or charity, a local, regional or national community, or a small, medium business or enterprise, building a formal partnership with a museum or collection, co-creating a workshop with a school or external organisation, engaging the public with research ideas, or helping to form public policy, knowledge exchange is a reciprocal act which helps both parties, and has both tangible and intangible outcomes.[7]

The same project hopes for numerous "pathways and outcomes" of these partnerships. No doubt, the effects or success rate of knowledge exchanges will considerably vary, depending, among many factors, on the disciplines and practices involved, and their traditions, notably of past exchanges. Be that as it may, a solid trend is being set.

Clearly, the fact that universities and research centres are highly committed partners in knowledge exchange processes does not exempt them from the need to launch a critical reflection on these concepts, also with regard to their own usages, such as the relations between science and knowledge, between theoretical and applied approaches, and issues like transfer of knowledge. One may identify three typical viewpoints with regard to knowledge aspects in scholarly discourse: an epistemological, a sociological and a historical viewpoint.

The first probes the basic features of knowledge, a concept covering, since the Greek, a number of different acts and skills: "*techne* (knowing how), *episteme* (knowing that), *praxis* (practice),

---

[6] Another example, among many more: the "Rencontres Recherche et Création" co-organized in July 2019 by the ANR (Agence nationale de la recherche), the Festival d'Avignon and the CNRS (https://www.recherche-creation-avignon.fr/, accessed on June 13, 2019).

[7] Oxford Research Centre in the Humanities, https://www.torch.ox.ac.uk/knowledge-exchange, accessed on 10 May 2019.

phronesis (prudence) and *gnosis* (insight)" (Burke, 2016: 14).[8] In addition, knowledge is culture-bound, varies in time and space, and appears in many kinds: "[...] knowledge is pure and applied, abstract and concrete, explicit and implicit, learned and popular, male and female, local and universal" (Burke, 2016: 14). Moreover, acts of knowledge are closely linked to other perceptions of the world, such as attitudes, feelings or beliefs, many of which may, to some extent, have relevance for processes of understanding.

The second viewpoint is sociologically oriented and, notably today, attempts at framing and interpreting the many uncertainties that go with the almost unbridled expansion of science and technology in the last decades. One of these uncertainties is the impervious complexity of many sciences, another the threat of short-sightedness that goes with the inevitable focus on ever smaller topics. For many, science itself or its self-proclaimed "progress" needs to be put into question, since it does not solve all the problems, while its ambition, and especially its technological and digital applications, may announce the end of many other tools that humans have designed since ancient times to understand themselves and the world they live in. After all, science and technology are social practices, with political and economic implications, as exemplified by Latour and Woolgar (1986) in their study of how scientific work is carried out in laboratories, how scientists cooperate, how scholarly practices relate with pragmatic and strategic concerns such as the publication of papers, the search for finances and other daily aspects of academic life. Knowledge may serve as an umbrella term to include the many social features of scholarship and counterbalance the illusion of 'pure' science.

The third viewpoint is historical. While knowledge exchanges bear on controversies of our time, historians are keen to observe that these exchanges have a long history, far beyond modern science (Lipphardt and David, 2011). However, it should not come as a surprise that the latter rarely interacts with its own past, on the

---

[8] To take another language, Chinese distinguishes between *zhishi* (knowledge) and *shixue* (knowhow), in addition to "a plethora of terms including *changshi* (common knowledge), *xuewen* (learning), *mijue* (secret know-how), and *famen* (Buddhist enlightenment)" (Judge, 2017: 183).

contrary, it rather tends to dismiss so-called pre-scientific knowledges. This dismissal is now being stemmed by upcoming *histories* of knowledge (*histoire des savoirs, Wissensgeschichte*), in which modern science is integrated in a longer history of intellectual undertakings. Obviously, the historical argument bases on epistemological distinctions and is fed by the sociological setting previously mentioned: "One of the social functions of historians is surely to help their fellow-citizens to see the problems of the present in a long-term perspective and so to avoid parochialism" (Burke, 2016: 11).

The historical viewpoint towards knowledge exchange will be the vantage one adopted here, while the subject matter will be knowledge on translation throughout history. For practical reasons, the term "translation knowledge" covers the many types of reflection on translation that have been gathered, structured, analysed and used throughout the ages, in many places and many languages, in the form of treaties, manuals, theories, criticism, methods, letters, prefaces, etc.[9]

As to "knowledge exchange," it is understood as a multidirectional process of interaction between knowledges on translation in other languages and cultures, as well as with different sorts of knowledge, such as social, religious, educational, literary, historical, or scientific ones. The term exchange is less ambiguous, perhaps, than "circulation," which might suggest that translation knowledge can be isolated from other knowledges, or "transfer," which might suggest that the process is unidirectional. At any rate, types of knowledge should always be historically contextualised.

Last but not least, while the long history of translation knowledge has rarely split between theory and practice (to use shortcut terms), it is undeniable that during the last decades thinking on translation has more radically than before distanced scientific approaches from one another and especially former knowledges, a distancing which has frequently prevented scholars

---

[9] Of course, the term includes implicit, sometimes non-written, types of knowledge, like the translator's know-how or poetics (see also D'hulst and Gambier, 2018).

from getting interested in the latter. However, one should also say that this state of affairs is rapidly changing, as it has already changed in numerous other disciplines (law, biology, medicine and more).

3. Histories of translation knowledge

It is encouraging to see that the growing interest in translation history has enabled the launching and completion of large enterprises in many languages and areas. Three models of presenting translations and their knowledges seem to prevail so far.[10]

The first adopts language as a unifying factor, giving way to histories of translations into single target languages.[11] One among many examples of such histories is *Suomennoskirjallisuuden historia* (*History of literary translation into Finnish*, Kovala et al., 2007). It seems to embrace the view, borrowed from national and comparative literature histories or, later on, polysystem studies, that translations written in the (major) language of the target culture (often a nation-state) share a number of formal, thematic or generic features with original language products of that target culture. Obviously, only intranslations into the target language share these features, not the extranslations made into other languages. By hypothesis, the preceding view seems to apply to translation knowledges that are produced in the same language within the same target culture. Examples here are Amos Ross' *Early Theories of translation* (1920), D'hulst's *Cent ans de théorie française de la traduction* (1990) or Tak-hung Chan's overview of *Twentieth-Century Chinese Translation Theory* (2004). Explicit justifications for language-based histories of translation knowledge are rarely given.

A variant of the single language model includes more areas that share that language and supposedly build a sort of language-based knowledge community, as occurs with labels such as

---

[10] When the scope is limited to histories of modern translation knowledges, more models may be mentioned, and these take into account other categories, such as change, mapping, genre and theme (D'hulst, 2020).
[11] More than histories of translations made out of a given source language.

Francophone, Hispanophone, Arabophone, Sinophone or Anglophone. Two examples of such a larger model are the five-volume *Oxford History of Literary Translation in English* covering all Anglophone regions of the world (France and Gillespie, 2006) and the recently achieved *Histoire des traductions en langue française* in four volumes that takes into account writings on translation into French being produced in Francophone areas outside France (Chevrel and Masson, 2012-2019). Another variant broadens the single-language scope by attempting to group languages into families or "traditions" (Germanic languages, Romance languages, etc., as with Gambier and Stecconi, 2019). Again, the idea of traditions tends to suggest corresponding knowledge communities.

The second model is more recent and less common than the previous one. It combines language and space in a number of configurations. The typical shape is the nation-state as a container of more than one target language. An example is Lafarga and Pejenaute's *Historia de la traducción en España* (2004): their history covers, successively, translations into Castilian, Catalan, Galician and Basque. Yet, translations *between* the latter are not considered, nor are extranslations out of these languages. Other histories include translations between the national or local languages of the nation-state. Examples here are Clements' work on *Translation in Early Modern Japan* (2015) and Kothari's *A Multilingual Nation. Translation and Language Dynamic in India* (2017).

Area approaches that open up for larger entities are scarce but are gaining ground, as witnessed by a recent *Histoire de la traduction littéraire en Europe médiane* (2019), in which Chalvin and others study the interaction through translation between several language communities and nation-states of Middle Europe. Obviously, a broader scope advantages the study of the dissemination of translation knowledges across larger distances and between more cultures, with the likelihood that knowledges on translation are themselves translated. Scopes may widen even more, as with Albrecht and Plack's *Europäische Übersetzungsgeschichte* (2019), which gives only a brief glance at knowledge production and exchange of knowledge across Europe. Comprehensive overviews or anthologies of translation and translation knowledge (amongst others Ballard, 2013; Robinson, 2014) hardly give proper consideration to exchange matters.

The most recent approach towards area studies "looks for new ways of conceptualizing linguistic and translational space beyond national languages and the boundaries of the nation-state" (Armstrong, 2019, s.p.). Two of these ways relate to the Early modern period in Europe (approx. 15th-18th centuries): a network analysis of agents (translators, authors, publishers, booksellers etc.) and, to a lesser extent, new GIS technologies (Geographic Information Technologies) geared to pinpoint multiscale trajectories (local, national, transnational ones). Both ways seem promising, yet the second is still in its embryonic stage, while none has so far produced studies of moving knowledges, or by extension, travelling theoreticians and other knowledge mediators.

The third and equally recent model is discipline-oriented, and investigates the role of translation in the international exchange of specific disciplinary knowledges, such as legal, medical, or biological ones. As the work of Montgomery (2000), Burke (2000-2012), Cook and Dupré (2012), Fransen, Hodson, and Enenkel (2017), to name but a few, has solidly documented, translation recasts the contents and formats of knowledge. Knowledge through translation being the key matter, knowledge on translation, once again, falls outside the main scope.

All in all, each model raises further questions. Take language-based histories: they mostly study a single translation direction (from source to target), while translation sociology has evidenced that one had better consider more directions, since languages are interdependent, a factor which influences translation flows from and into these languages (van Es and Heilbron, 2015). Admittedly, the dissemination of translation knowledges during the past has benefited from the influential position occupied by languages like Latin, Arabic, French, Spanish, Russian, or Chinese. However, the latter consistently interacted with other languages.

Conversely, looking at area-based histories from the vantage point of knowledge exchange may help to avoid the risk of over-emphasizing the self-sufficiency of nation-states as containers or "owners" of ideas, as well as the idiosyncrasy of individual scholars.[12] How language-bound are ideas on translation originally written in a given language? And what about the "national" qualification of ideas expressed by, say, travelling "Flemish" scholars that wrote in English, and have lived and worked in the UK or the US?

Needless to say, the issue of knowledge exchange calls for further modelling: one may think of introducing additional parameters, such as public and private institutions that steer and control the transmission of translation knowledge, or market conditions and cultural contexts that advantage specific types of knowledge. At this point, it seems, the trouble is less to substantiate the importance of a study of knowledge exchanges than to find adequate ways of mapping these exchanges. This is the topic of the next section.

4. A focus on exchange of translation knowledge

Patent tools to exchange translation knowledge are direct import and export, indirect transfer operations (reviews, quotations, paraphrases, summaries), and translations proper of books, essays, manuals and other texts on translation knowledge that are published or spread otherwise.[13] How should one map these exchanges with the aim of uncovering patterns or trends, while keeping track with the models of translation history that we have just discussed? One possible way to proceed is to define anchor points on large axes that have proven their historical significance, for instance with regard to social, scientific or cultural practices or disciplines that make use of translation. One may think of centres vs. peripheries, local vs. global knowledges, openings vs. closures towards external practices, reciprocal exchanges, continuities vs.

---

[12] A bias that naturally extends far beyond translation proper, as with legal systems: "Should a non-European legal system that has taken up French law be conceived, for instance, as belonging to the Roman legal family, or should it rather be located within the legal family to which the surrounding legal systems belonged? Often, the ultimate aim of such studies was to estimate the impact that one's own legal order had in the world" (Foljanty, 2015: 2).

[13] E.g. orally in pre-print periods, but also during conferences, via teaching, or by means of audio-visual carriers, Internet and the like.

changes, etc. By way of examples, the next sections offer a brief depiction of three such axes.[14]

Centres and peripheries

Hegemonic societies have disseminated their ideologies, rules and cultural practices with the help of translation. All the same, they have conveyed their views on translation itself, as Rome did by means of its methods for grammar and especially writing, in which translation has the crucial function of imitating and emulating Greek genres (Copeland, 1995). From the Middle Ages on, colonial regimes made use of translation to disseminate their languages and worldviews, as happened with the famous *Ratio studiorum* (1599), i.e. the Jesuit code of liberal education pervading Europe (Italy, Spain, Portugal, Austria, France, Germany, etc.) and numerous colonies (amongst others India, Cuba, Mexico, and the Philippines), at least up until the end of the 18th century.

Similar cases of centre-periphery relations with regard to knowledge exchange can be found in later periods, such as the French Revolution and Napoleonic Empire (D'hulst and Schreiber, 2014), the Habsburg period (Wolf, 2012), Fascism (Rundle, 2010), and even extend to the diffusion of translation theories in former Eastern Europe during Soviet communism (Tyulenev and Nuriev, 2020). All witness the rulers' sensitive understanding and mobilising of translation as an efficient way to disseminate new ideologies, publicize laws and regulations, or convey military propaganda. Grafted on an ingenious management of media, translations were often printed side by side with the original, the logical and chronological pre-eminence of which is thus emphasized.

Reciprocal exchanges

Centre-periphery relations easily recall the well-known sociology-based analyses of contemporary translation flows and may

---

[14] Space limits prevent us from dwelling upon the lengthy historiographical and epistemological debates that most categories have raised.

therefore be viewed as tokens of an intellectual environment in which languages are considered as discrete units commonly equated with nation-states or clusters of states fitting the historical self-understanding of Western societies. The latter, in particular, has yielded alternative histories of knowledge production and exchange in which European or Western translation studies underwent a process of "provincialisation" (Kothari, 2014: 98) within a more variegated picture of the world, featuring "practices of thought emerging from lived conditions of a multilingual nation"[15] (Kothari, *ibid.*). Also, less conspicuous relations, like Arabic into Latin exchanges arising during the long Abbasid period between the 8th and 13th century (Hasse, 2006), counterbalanced one-sided views and confirm the historical intermingling of different knowledge exchange processes.

More fundamentally, perhaps, in many if not most known cases, the imposition of central views has encountered resistance in dominated or occupied societies and their languages, and has been questioned and even replaced by new understandings of translation, which have in turned made their way into more central languages or societies. For example, the tactics of resistance against colonial worldviews, as documented by Gruzinski (1999) with regard to 16th- and 17th-century hybridizing translation views and techniques elaborated in Mexico, has received further expansion in postcolonial translation studies. A similar expansion applies to the view, shaped in many multilingual countries, like Belgium during the 19th century, that translation is a powerful tool to voice and promote dominated languages, i.e. Flemish in the example of Belgium.

To sum up, the centre-periphery model is put to the test by interactive views, which do not only focus to a greater extent on "resistances, inertias and [...] new combinations" (Werner and Zimmermann, 2006: 38), but emphasize also that the imposition of central knowledges always relies on the acknowledgment of local knowledges.

---

[15] In this case India.

Continuities and changes

Referring to Fernand Braudel's well-known distinction between three timescales or "durées" (Braudel, 1949; see also Rundle, 2018, and Wakabayashi, 2019a), one may argue that translation knowledge features long-term views as well as cyclical and short-term ones. In Europe, long-term views have clustered ideas about translation as a mode of learning deeply engrained in two disciplines, i.e. grammar and rhetoric (from the Roman period until the 19th century, as studied by Rener, 1989). Similarly, models for translating Indian Buddhist texts in China have monitored strictly conventionalized procedures from the 2nd century to the 15th century at least (Zacchetti, 2019). Alternatively, popular views on translation have found expression in countless and lasting metaphors, catch phrases and stereotypes, such as "the letter and the spirit," "translation and smuggling," *traduttore traditore*, etc. (Delisle, 2017). These views have sprawled in Europe and beyond, but almost invisibly, it seems. Like memes of translation (Chesterman, 2016), their properties and transformations are as hard to observe as their transmission.[16]

Concomitantly, history witnesses recurring or cyclical types of translation knowledge, such as the search for language universals, the idea of cultural translation, the opposition between imitation and emulation, the need for retranslations, the rhetoric of linear progress and improvement (Belle, 2014) and so on. Once again, translation historians have rarely set out to study the spread of such knowledges across national or linguistic traditions. Obviously, "historical trajectories as those of Western cultures [...] are by no means 'natural' or universal. Rather than lagging behind the West, other cultures might simply be following a different path" (Wakabayashi, 2019a: 26). In other terms, different sets of cyclical knowledges coexist and probably also intermingle.

Unexpectedly, perhaps, research on long-term and mid-term knowledge exchanges remains underrepresented in comparison with research on short-term views, which have their strongest

---

[16] Hence, the scarcity of historical studies devoted to translation memetics.

resonance in modern and contemporary views on translation. Short-term views seem to have become a characteristic feature of the evolution of translation studies over the last 50 years. Think of the successive linguistic, cultural, postcolonial, sociological, historical and audio-visual turns put forward in British and North-American scholarship on translation and frequently taken over in introductions on translation that spread in other and smaller languages (D'hulst, 2020).

If anchor points can be drawn in for the study of exchanges across linguistic and geopolitical borders, they may as well prove fruitful for restricted language-bound and area-bound approaches. For instance, the recently achieved *Histoire des traductions en langue française* by Chevrel and Masson (2012-2019) allows future researchers to foster a long-term transversal perspective on the history of French translation theories and to observe if or to what extent the meaning of basic concepts like "traduction," "retraduction," "pseudo-traduction," "adaptation," "imitation," etc. has altered during their transmission between generations. Adding an interlingual perspective makes it possible to explore how such concepts, or the theories they are part of, combined the import of long-term views on translation, like the Roman, with the import of short-term ones, like the British and Italian writings by Dryden, Pope, Monti or Cesarotti during the 18th and 19th centuries. In this respect, it becomes all the more interesting to confront knowledge exchanges with the lack thereof, as occurred with the German Romantic theories by Goethe or Schleiermacher which French thinkers have hardly picked up during the same period.

All the same, exchanges taking place on different scales are no less relevant topics for study than the crossing of transnational borders. Take the already mentioned hegemonic Habsburg or French translation policies: they have usually been replicated with modifications at the lower scale of the many language communities under their administration, but also within provinces, cities and municipalities, as has been prospected for a set of European towns during the 19th century (D'hulst and Koskinen, 2020).

To further relate, compare or contrast translation knowledges of different sorts and shapes is a task within reach of the next generation. Yet, when it comes to focus on exchanges between more languages and covering longer distances, including continents, the cross-cultural approaches that have their centre of gravity in a single nation-state, target language or cultural area run the risk of falling short. Even if national frames remain crucial to understanding knowledge exchanges, it does not suffice to pile up national translation histories nor juxtapose European or Eurocentric approaches and postcolonial ones that have actively invested in the construction and exchange of alternative knowledges to achieve that end. The fact is that during their long history knowledges have more than once interconnected at a universal scale.

5. By way of a conclusion

An overarching view on the exchange of translation knowledge is better served when it is in line with the priorities of world history as a discipline:

> As it has developed since the 1960s and particularly since the 1980s, the new world history has focused attention on comparisons, connections, networks, and systems rather than the experiences of individual communities or discrete societies. (Bentley, 2011: 2)

Comparisons, connections, networks, and systems: such a programme is most challenging with regard to a history of translation knowledges, in particular when bearing in mind that data are lacking for many societies and periods, that historians are less numerous in Africa than in Europe or the United States, and that long-distance connections between knowledges produced in different parts of the world still have to be uncovered. Not to forget that methodological matters need proper consideration: how may one come to terms with different historical metalanguages (Gambier, 2019) and different periodization systems (Lorenz, 2017)? How should one describe, interpret and compare knowledges born and transmitted in quite different material and symbolic worlds, before and after print? In other terms, how should one pass from a "De-Westernized" to an international history of translation knowledges (Heller, 2019)?

This is the utopia of such a history: an impossible undertaking and, paradoxically, one that might prove indispensable in the longer run, not only in view of curbing the sterile geopolitical and intellectual compartmentalization of translation studies in East and West or North and South, but also of underpinning the continuous quest for the fundamentals of translational communication. This quest includes the understanding of the genesis and growth of the translation concept itself, which needs a thorough sort of connective and comparative thinking. One may hope that coming histories of knowledge, as sustained by Renn (2012), Benjamin (2014), Adelman (2019), and others, will provide ample space for connective histories of translation knowledge with a sufficiently ample scale.[17] At a moment when global science threatens diversity in thinking, historians of knowledge may very well be the true guardians of the interconnected diversity across the world.

References

Adelman, Jeremy. *Empire and the Social Sciences: Global Histories of Knowledge*. London: Bloomsbury, 2019.

Agost, Rosa. "Translation Studies and the mirage of a lingua franca." *Perspectives*, 23/2 (2015): 249-264.

Albrecht, Jörn, and René Métrich, eds. *Manuel de traductologie*. Berlin: de Gruyter, 2016.

Albrecht, Jörn, and Iris Plack. *Europäische Übersetzungsgeschichte*. Tübingen: Gunter Narr Verlag, 2018.

Amos Ross, Flora. *Early Theories of Translation*. New York: Columbia University Press, 1920.

Armstrong, Guyda. "Towards a Spatial Early Modern Translation Studies." *InTRAlinea*, 21 (2019): 1-10.

Ballard, Michel. *Histoire de la traduction. Repères historiques et culturels*. Bruxelles: De Boeck Supérieur, 2013.

---

[17] Cf. Drayton and Motadel: "Global history is not a federation of national and area studies history, as important and sovereign as these levels of analysis are. It is the product of engagements with the problem of the global, based on inspired comparative and connective thinking and not just the accumulation of examples from different regions" (2018: 15).

Banoun, Bernard, and Isabelle Poulin. "L'Âge de la traduction (1914-2000)." In Bernard Banoun, Isabelle Poulin, and Yves Chevrel, eds. *Histoire des traductions en langue française. XXᵉ siècle (1914-2000)*. Paris: Verdier, 2019: 39-54.

Belle, Marie-Alice. "At the Interface between Translation History and Literary History: A Genealogy of the Theme of 'Progress' in Seventeenth-century English Translation History and Criticism." *The Translator*, 20/1 (2014): 44-63.

Benjamin, Craig. "'But from this time forth history becomes a connected whole': State Expansion and the Origins of Universal History." *Journal of Global History*, 9/3 (2014): 357-378.

Bentley, Jerry H. "Cross-Cultural Interaction and Periodization in World History." *The American Historical Review*, 101/3 (1996): 749-770.

Bentley, Jerry H. "The Task of World History." In Jerry H. Bentley, ed. *The Oxford Handbook of World History*. Oxford: Oxford University Press, 2011: 1-16.

Blakesley, Jacob. "Examining Modern European Poet-Translators 'Distantly.'" *Translation and Literature*, 25/1 (2016): 10-27.

Braudel, Fernand. *La Méditerranée et le monde méditerranéen à l'époque de Philippe II*. Paris: Armand Colin, 1949.

Burke, Peter. *What is the History of Knowledge?* Cambridge: Polity Press, 2016.

Burke, Peter, and Ronnie Po-chia Hsia, eds. *Cultural Translation in Early Modern Europe*. Cambridge: Cambridge University Press, 2007.

Chalvin, Antoine, Jean-Léon Muller, Katre Taviste, and Marie Vrinat-Nikolov, eds. *Histoire de la traduction littéraire en Europe médiane. Des origines à 1989*. Rennes: Presses Universitaires de Rennes, 2019.

Chesterman, Andrew. *Memes of Translation. The Spread of Ideas in Translation Theory*. Amsterdam: John Benjamins, 2016.

Chevrel, Yves, and Jean-Yves Masson, eds. *Histoire des traductions en langue française*. Paris: Verdier, 4 vol., 2012-2019.

Christian, David. "Introduction and Overview." In David Christian, ed. *The Cambridge World History*. Vol 1. Cambridge: Cambridge University Press, 2015: 1-38.

Clements, Rebekah. *A Cultural History of Translation in Early Modern Japan*. Cambridge: Cambridge University Press, 2015.

Copeland, Rita. *Rhetoric, Hermeneutics, and Translation in the Middle Ages: Academic Traditions and Vernacular Texts*. Cambridge: Cambridge University Press, 1995.

Cook, Harold John, and Sven Dupré. *Translating Knowledge in the Early Modern Low Countries*. Münster: LIT Verlag, 2012.

Dahui, Dong, and Meng-Lin Chen. "Publication Trends and Co-Citation Mapping of Translation Studies between 2000 and 2015." *Scientometrics*, 105 (2015): 1111-1128.

De León, Celia Martín. "Metaphorical Models of Translation: Transfer vs Imitation and Action." In James St. André, ed. *Thinking Through Translation with Metaphors*. Manchester: St. Jerome Publishing, 2010: 75-108.

Delisle, Jean. *La traduction en citations: Florilège*. Ottawa: Presses de l'Université Ottawa, 2017.

Delisle, Jean, and Judith Woodsworth, eds. *Translators through History*. Revised edition. Amsterdam, Philadelphia: John Benjamins, 2012.

D'hulst, Lieven. *Cent ans de théorie française de la traduction. De Batteux à Littré (1748-1847)*. Lille: Presses Universitaires du Septentrion, 1990.

D'hulst, Lieven. "The History of Translation Studies as a Discipline." In Christopher Rundle, ed. *The Routledge Handbook of Translation History*. Abingdon: Routledge, 2021: 3-22.

D'hulst, Lieven. "Un regard d'historien sur les échanges des savoirs traductifs." In Nicolas Froeliger, Christian Balliu, and Mathilde Fontanet, eds. *Traduction et traductologie: la fin de l'histoire?* In print (2022).

D'hulst, Lieven, and Yves Gambier, eds. *A History of Modern Translation Knowledge. Sources, Concepts, Effects*. Amsterdam, Philadelphia: John Benjamins, 2018.

D'hulst, Lieven, and Kaisa Koskinen, eds. *Translating in Town. Local Translation Policies During the European 19th Century*. London: Bloomsbury, 2020.

Drayton, Richard, and David Motadel. "Discussion: The Futures of Global History." *Journal of Global History*, 13 (2018): 1-21.

Foljanty, Lena. "Legal Transfers as Processes of Cultural Translation: On the Consequences of a Metaphor." *Max Planck Institute for European Legal History*, research paper series, 9 (2015): 1-18.

France, Peter, and Stuart Gillespie, eds. *The Oxford History of Literary Translation in English*. Oxford: Oxford University Press, 5 vol., 2006-.

Franco Aixelà, Javier. *BITRA (Bibliography of Interpreting and Translation)*. Open-access bibliographical database. 2001-2018. http://doi.org/10.14198/bitra

Franco Aixelà, Javier. "Who's Who and What's What in Translation Studies: A preliminary approach." In Catherine Way, Sonia Vandepitte, Reine Meylaerts, and Magdalena Bartłomiejczyk, eds. *Tracks and Treks in Translation Studies*. Amsterdam: John Benjamins, 2013: 7-28.

Fransen, Sietske, Niall Hodson, and Karl A.E. Enenkel, eds. *Translating Early Modern Science*. Leiden: Brill, 2017.

Gambier, Yves, and Ubaldo Stecconi, eds. *A World Atlas of Translation*. Amsterdam, Philadelphia: John Benjamins, 2019.

Gruzinski, Serge. *La pensée métisse*. Paris: Éditions Fayard, 1999.

Hasse, Dag Nikolaus. "The Social Conditions of the Arabic- (Hebrew-) Latin Translation Movements in Medieval Spain and in the Renaissance." In Andreas Speer, and Lydia Wegener, eds. *Wissen über Grenzen: Arabisches Wissen und Lateinisches Mittelalter*. Berlin: Walter de Gruyter, 2006: 68-88.

Heilbron, Johan, Gustavo Sora, and Thibaud Boncourt, eds. *The Social and Human Sciences in Global Power Relations*. London: Palgrave Macmillan, 2018.

Heller, Lavinia. "De-Westernize! Historisierung und (Inter)Kulturalisierung translationswissenschaftlicher Diskurse." In Lavinia Heller, and Tomasz Rozmysłowicz, eds. *Translation und interkulturelle Kommunikation. Beträge zur Theorie, Empirie und Praxis kultureller Austauschprozesse. Translation and Intercultural Communication. Theoretical, Empirical and Practical Perspectives on Cultural Exchanges*. Berlin: Frank & Timme, 2019: 37-50.

Judge, Joan. "Review of Burke 2016." *Canadian Journal of History*, 52:1 (2017): 182-184.

Kothari, Rita. "Response." *Translation Studies*, 7:1 (2014): 96-99.

Kothari, Rita, ed. *A Multilingual Nation. Translation and Language Dynamic in India*. Oxford: Oxford University Press, 2017.

Kovala, Urpo, Pekka Kujamäki, Outi Paloposki, and H.K. Riikonen, eds. *Suomennoskirjallisuuden historia*, 1-2 [History of literary translation into Finnish 1-2]. Helsinki: SKS, 2007.

Lässig, Simone. "The History of Knowledge and the Expansion of the Historical Research Agenda." *Bulletin of the GHI*, 59 (2016): 29–58.

Lafarga, Francisco, and Luis Pegenaute, eds. *Historia de la traducción en España*. Salamanca: Almar, 2004.

Lipphardt, Veronika, and Ludwig David. "Knowledge Transfer and Science Transfer." *European History Online*, published by the Institute of European History (IEG), Mainz, 2011. URL: http://www.ieg-ego.eu/lipphardtv-ludwigd-2011-en. Accessed on 15 March 2020.

Montgomery, Scott L. *Science in Translation: Movements of Knowledge through Cultures and Time*. Chicago: University of Chicago Press, 2000.

Rener, Frederic. *Interpretatio: Language and Translation from Cicero to Tytler*. Amsterdam: Rodopi, 1989.

Renn, Jürgen. *The Globalization of Knowledge in History*. Berlin: Edition Open Access, 2012.

Robinson, Douglas. *Western Translation Theory from Herodotus to Nietzsche*. Abingdon: Routledge, 2014.

Rovira-Esteva, Sara, and Javier Franco Aixelà (2018). "Bibliometric Tools. Evaluation, Mapping." In Lieven D'hulst and Yves Gambier, eds., *A History of Modern Translation Knowledge, op. cit.*: 117-122.

Rovira-Esteva, Sara, Javier Franco Aixelà, and Christian Olalla-Soler. "Citation Patterns in Translation Studies: a Format-Dependent Bibliometric Analysis." *Translation & Interpreting*, 11:1 (2019): 147-171.

Rundle, Christopher. "Translation in Fascist Italy: 'The Invasion of Translations.'" In Christopher Rundle, and Kate Sturge, eds. *Translation Under Fascism*. London: Palgrave Macmillan, 2010: 15-50.

Rundle, Christopher (2018). "Temporality." In Lieven D'hulst, and Yves Gambier, eds., *A History of Modern Translation Knowledge, op. cit.*: 235-245.

Tyulenev, Sergey, and Vitaly Nuriev. "'Sewing up' the Soviet Politico-cultural System: Translation in the Multilingual USSR." In Andy Byford, Connor Doak, and Stephen Hutchings, eds. *Transnational Russian Studies*. Liverpool: Liverpool University Press, 2020: 155-168.

Vandaele, Sylvie. "Les traductions françaises de *The Origin of Species*: approche lexicométrique." *Hermēneus. Revista de Traducción e Interpretación*, 21 (2019): 387-422.

van Es, N., and Johan Heilbron. "Fiction from the Periphery: How Dutch Writers Enter the Field of English-Language Literature." *Cultural Sociology*, 9:3 (2015): 296-319.

Wakabayashi, Judy (2019a). "Time Matters: Conceptual and Methodological Considerations in Translation Timescapes." *Chronotopos*, 1 (2019): 22-39.

Wakabayashi, Judy (2019b). "Digital Approaches to Translation History." *Translation & Interpreting*, 11:2 (2019): 132-145.

Werner, Michael, and Bénédicte Zimmermann. "Beyond Comparison: *Histoire croisée* and the Challenge of Reflexivity." *History and Theory*, 45:1 (2006): 30-50.

Zacchetti, Stefano. "Translation Theories and Practices in Medieval Chinese Buddhism." Unpublished conference given at Treviso, Venice, on *Translation History and Translation Stories* (15-16 April 2019).

Comparative Literature: A Revitalization

Joseph Pivato (Athabasca University, Canada)

In this paper I argue that Comparative Literature in the English-speaking world can be revitalized by focusing on the study and use of different languages. To my argument I bring my Canadian experiences with multiculturalism and practices of bilingualism. I contrast these methodologies with the American trends of unilingual English practice and the dependence on texts in English translation.

Comparative Literature in North America is under attack. As literary studies become more and more dominated by unilingual English departments, students and academics are in danger of getting only a single perspective on literary works and literary questions. Texts in English translation are often inadequate. As bilingual Canadians have known for many years you cannot translate everything into English.

Here are some examples of problems with English translations. When we translate a canonical Italian novel such as Alessandro Manzoni's *I Promesi Sposi* into English, are we creating an English novel, or some kind of hybrid? How do we read this novel outside its cultural context? How do we understand this novel if we have no knowledge of Italian language, culture and history? To cite another example: how do you translate Charles Baudelaire's *Les Fleurs du Mal* into English? We find that English translations often produce a very limited understanding of the original text and a simplified view of the literature. Modernism in France is not the same as modernism in England.

There are also particular problems with translating European theorists such as Derrida, Barthes, Foucault or Julia Kristeva into English. These writers often use their original languages in complex ways and experiment with terms and ideas. How does an American translate Derrida's use of the term *differance*? Is it by the term "difference" or by the term "deferral"? Can the translation be:

"Different meanings are deferred"? Do we understand that behind this playful term, *differance* is Derrida's arguments against the phenomenology of Edmund Husserl? In my experience American English translations tend to simplify the language and reduce terms to the undergraduate level of discourse. I could list many more examples of the shortcomings of English translations.

In Canada from the beginning Comparative Literature study has been bilingual, English and French, and in the 1990s has expanded to include the other languages spoken in Canada. This is demonstrated by the establishment of programs in Comparative Canadian Literature which study French-Canadian authors and English-Canadian writers along with those of diverse ethnic origins. Many European readers can appreciate this diversity.

In contrast to this, the American approach to Comparative Literature has focused on European canonical texts in English translation. This unilingual American approach to Comparative Literature is reflected in the reports published by the American Comparative Literature Association and by the practice of offering Comparative Literature courses in English departments by unilingual faculty members. University administrators have argued that all this graduate work can be done in English, and there is no need for Comparative Literature programs or courses in foreign languages. One example of this is that the important Comparative Literature program at the University of North Carolina at Chapel Hill was absorbed into the English Department. In the last two decades many American literature programs for both graduate and undergraduate degrees have eliminated the foreign language requirements. Examples of this trend are the State University of New York at Albany, Louisiana State University, the University of Maine, the University of Minnesota, the University of Nevada, George Washington University and the University of Wisconsin (Foderaro, 2010).[1]

---

[1] In addition to Lisa W. Foderaro's article about drastic cuts to language progams in many American universities there is the 2019 report of the Modern Language Association of American by Dennis Looney & Natalia Lisin, "Enrollments in Languages Other Than English in United States Institutions of Higher Learning (Summer 2016 and Fall 2016)" which states that the number of language

In the decade of the 2020s Comparative Literature can be the study of almost any kind of writing or of different art forms since they can all be read as types of discourse. With the consideration of conceptual art, performance art and written expression beyond genres, comparative study has expanded to the point where it is no longer necessary to explain the need for transmedia storytelling. Then we find that there is a controversy between transmedia and intermedia (Newman). This question itself can become the focus of a comparative study. Trends and theories in literary study such as intersectionality and the post-human are changing so quickly that it is difficult to develop a program in comparative study, let alone an introductory text. Despite this diversity in media and texts I argue that we need the knowledge of languages beyond English.

The fact that in the 1990s few English texts in the field of comparative literary studies were written and published is an indication of the on-going crisis in Comparative Literature. A condition which Linda Hutcheon identified as "this 'anxiogenic' state of Comparative Literature in North America—in Canada as much as in the United States" (Hutcheon, 1996: 35)

Beginning in the 1960s the American Comparative Literature Association conducted periodic reviews of the state of the discipline and published the results. The first was "The Levin Report, 1965: Report on Professional Standards." The second was "The Greene Report, 1975: A Report on Standards." The third, "The Bernheimer Report, 1993: Comparative Literature at the Turn of the Century," was expanded into a volume with contributions by sixteen American comparatists: *Comparative Literature in the Age of Multiculturalism* (1995), ed. Charles Bernheimer. This format was followed with the Saussy report, *Comparative Literature in an Age of Globalization* (2006), ed. Haun Saussy. The most recent ACLA report was first posted online in March 2014 with added content until April, 2015. The final paper version, *Futures of Comparative Literature: ACLA State of the Discipline Report* (2017) was edited by

---

programs offered in Fall 2016 was down by 651 programs since 2013. The complete report is available online.

Ursula K. Heise with the help of several other American comparatists.

In the Bernheimer anthology of 1995 the identity crisis in Comparative Literature becomes painfully apparent. In this collection many contributors down-played language study from a unilingual American point of view, misrepresented or misunderstood multiculturalism and were sceptical even of theory, seeing it as a possible dead end. Bernheimer expresses his own disenchantment in his introduction:

> Anxiety was fashionable. Indeed, it was *de rigueur*, rigor being the fetish of theory. But, as the Regan-Bush years gradually eroded the liberal agenda, it became more and more painful for many professors in literature departments to continue in an attitude of sceptical detachment and sophisticated alienation. The inevitable aporia of deconstructive undecidability began to seem too much like the indecipherable double-talk of the politicians we detested. Even those, myself included, who had been deeply influenced by deconstruction were feeling tired of systematic, suspicious vigilance, tired and demoralized by the work of displacing the ground from under our own feet, tired of being morally rigorous, tired of comparisons that always collapsed into indifference. (Bernheimer: 5)

All too many of the contributors to this volume also express doubts and pessimism. Tobin Siebers is blunt in his criticism,

> To my mind, there is no doubt that Comparative Literature as a discipline is dying. The irony is that it is being wrecked by its own success… Comparatists are losing their identity in the university because everyone is becoming a comparatist of a kind. (Siebers: 196)

In the phrase "everyone is becoming a comparatist" is the assumption and belief that students can read works from all the literatures of the world in English translation with little knowledge of different languages or cultures. With the exception of Mary Louise Pratt and Rey Chow, the other contributors to the Bernheimer volume seem to support this unilingual approach to comparative study. The paradox of the general American resistance towards learning another language at a time of global education is explored by Peter N. Stearns in *Educating Global Citizens in Colleges and Universities* (2008).

It soon becomes clear that the subtext to this general malaise in the Bernheimer collection was the Culture Wars of the 1990s. There were few new books produced in Comparative Literature in that decade but there were nine books published on the Culture Wars beginning with James Davidson Hunter's *The Culture Wars: The Struggle to Define America* (1992). These books identify a number of polarizing issues in the Culture Wars such as immigration, multiculturalism, and the teaching and use of foreign languages. It is possible that because of these polarizing conflicts many of the contributors do not directly address questions such as multiculturalism in any open and creative manner. American politicians have contributed to the divisive battles on these and many other related issues; the result is a chill on open discussion on these ethnic and racial issues.

Mary Louise Pratt is the only academic in the Bernheimer collection who openly challenges the unilingual tendencies in the America academy. Her words read like a manifesto for Comparative Literature:

> Comparative Literature should remain the home for polyglots; multilingualism and polyglossia should remain its calling card. But it might help to update our rhetoric on this issue. Instead of producing students who "know foreign languages," maybe we should start talking about producing *bilingual, bicultural* people (or multilingual, multicultural people). Maybe we should link our endeavours to the need for deeply informed, culturally competent individuals in a globalizing world. This seems a good moment to reverse the United States' blind commitment to monolingualism and the tendency to cede the terrain of "globalization" to English. To monolingual Anglophones it may look like everyone in the world is learning English, but the more accurate statement, visible from where I stand, is that the world is becoming increasingly multilingual. Many people learn a kind of instrumental English as an international lingua franca. But Anglophones place themselves at a great disadvantage if they rely solely on this medium to conduct their relations with the rest of the planet. (Pratt: 62)

We should note that Mary Louise Pratt was born in, and had a bilingual education in, Canada, though she spent the rest of her career teaching in the United States.

In her 2003 book *Death of a Discipline* Gayatri Spivak was responding to the growing tendency toward monolingualism in the American academy. Spivak was calling for more protection for multiplicity of languages and literatures. She lost no time and began her arguments on the acknowledgements page itself:

> Publishing conglomerates have recognized a market for anthologies of world literature in translation. Academics with large advances are busy putting these together... Notes and introductions are provided by a scholar from the area commissioned for the purpose by the general editor, located in the United States. The market is international. Students in Taiwan and Nigeria will learn about the literature of the world through English translations organized by the United States (Spivak: xii).

Spivak recognized that she was going against the stream, but nevertheless called for resistance: "One can write in the hope that there may be some in the academy who do not believe that the critical edge of the humanities should be appropriated and determined by the market" (Spivak: xii). I agree with Spivak who questions the quality of these publications.

Haun Saussy's volume from 2006 was more hopeful in the diverse points of view it presented. Contributors either explicitly or implicitly called for the study of different languages and literatures beyond the European cannon. In her short essay Linda Hutcheon argued that Comparative Literature was congenitally contrarian and gave a Canadian explanation,

> I live in a country that shares a contrarian identity with the discipline I study. Like comparative literature, Canada is intensely self-reflexive – another way of saying that it has a persistent identity crisis, or at least persistent doubts about how to talk about itself. It too is founded historically upon exile, immigration and displacement. (Hutcheon, 2006: 228)

Despite this modest example from Canada's bilingualism and the obsession with self-interrogation, the Saussy volume was dominated by American points of view about every aspect of Comparative Literature. The call for more language study is expressed by a few voices crying in the wilderness of American monolingualism.

When Ursula Heise put together the online postings for *Futures of Comparative Literature: ACLA State of the Discipline Report* (2017), she included 53 short essays that seem to cover every possible topic related to Comparative Literature. The editor claims that this is the latest word on these topics; however, the points of view are predominantly American and often have not changed much since 1995. Seventeen of the short articles are between 600 and 700 words long and read like items from a reference book on literary terms.[2]

Two professors from UCLA produced a volume in 2011 to promote comparative literary studies. *A Companion to Comparative Literature*, edited by Ali Behdad and Dominic Thomas, includes thirty essays on topics such as literary theory, translation, gender and cultural formation, postcolonial studies, national literatures, migration, East-West encounters, and the impact of new media on literature. This text is aimed at American students since it is full of references to the society and history of that nation. Essays consider the history of Comparative Literature in America, racial questions, the American imagination, and Hollywood personalities like Marilyn Monroe. Many of the contributors are also found in the Saussy text and in the Heise anthology so we have similar American points of view repeated with little variation.

In my brief review I will include one more American book. These volumes give us a snapshot of the current state on Comparative Literature in North America. If a reader wants more details about any aspect of the field and the theories I would refer her or him to the volume *Introducing Comparative Literature: New Trends and Applications* (2015), by two professors, César Dominguez and Dario Villanueva, who work in Spain. The third author is Haun Saussy who comes from the University of Chicago. The text is meant as a thorough introduction for students and goes into much detail on any topic related to comparative study, literary history and theories. There is much discussion and many examples from European literature and from some other parts of the world; however, the commentary always refers back to American writers, scholars, publications and cultural artefacts. The American

---

[2] Ursula Heise's *Future of Comparative Literature* includes 53 articles, some of which are inadequate. In the section on translation Gayatri Spivak's note on language is only 420 words long and Shaden Tageldin's note on untranslatability is only 600 words long. Other examples are "periodization," 700 words, "philology," 600 words, "postcolonial studies," 653 words.

perspective is dominant here so the focus is on questions about theory rather than language study. In this 190-page book there is only one reference to Canadian comparatists. On the further reading list on page 149 the authors include Linda Hutcheon and Mario Valdés, editors of *Rethinking Literary History: A Dialogue on Theory* (2002).

While we may disagree with the unilingual approach to graduate studies in Comparative Literature that seems to be espoused by many academics in North America, we can agree that the discipline needs to be revitalized. One of the ways of revitalizing this discipline is to produce new books to promote it in the context of language studies. A bilingual country like Canada is an appropriate place to undertake this mission. Academics in Canada have done little in the last decade to promote Comparative Literature. We have an active Canadian Comparative Literature Association, but few publications directly in the field. The first time the CCLA published a survey of the state of Comparative Literature in Canada was in 1996 in a bilingual issue of the *Canadian Review of Comparative Literature* (23.1) guest-edited by Jonathan Hart. In 2009 the *Canadian Review of Comparative Literature* (36.1), guest-edited by Albert Braz and Marie Carrière, devoted the issue to Comparative Canadian Literature by including six essays in English or French. In 2014 the *Canadian Review of Comparative Literature* devoted part of an issue to the state of the field in Canada with a brief survey of fourteen graduate students and recent graduates from Comparative Literature programs (41.2). This last survey leads me, in part, to the arguments below.

We need a volume produced in Canada, by Canadian academics which presents Canadian perspectives on Comparative Literature and on questions about language study, multiculturalism, translations, women writers, ethnic minority writers, literature and film, literary theory, literary traditions, genres and a number of other topics. I have found that Canadians have many more views in common with Europeans than with Americans.

Consider the topic of translation, for example. Canadian students and academics have a better understanding of the problems with translation than American or British readers. Canada has a higher percentage of people who speak or read a second language than the USA or the UK. This better grasp of a second language and the questions of translation is reflected in the *Canadian Review of Comparative Literature* and its many different thematic issues and articles.

We find the phenomenon of self-translation among some English-Canadian and Quebec writers such as Daniel Gagnon, Antonio D'Alfonso, Erin Moure, Lica Canton, Patricia Smart and Nancy Huston. This is not a practice that normally occurs in the USA.

English-language textbooks on Comparative Literature are dominated by American academics and present American points of view and biases on all of the topics listed above. This is evident in the ACLA reports, in the volumes edited by Charles Bernheimer, Ali Behad, César Dominguez, and others. A Canadian text promoting Comparative Literature would need to address some of the American statements being promulgated with universal authority. The Canadian understanding and experience with multiculturalism is quite different from that of Americans who often view it as a social and cultural problem rather than an opportunity to learn about ethnic differences and languages. As Mary Louise Pratt pointed out above, many Americans think that they can understand the world through English translation. The Canadian-born French writer Nancy Huston practices self-translation between French and English as part of her creative process. Yet she makes these critical observations about the limits of translation:

> Le problème, voyez-vous, c'est que les langues ne sont pas seulement des langues; ce sont aussi des *world views*, c'est-à-dire des façons de voir et de comprendre le monde. Il y a de l'intraduisible là-dedans... (Huston: 51)

Most texts on Comparative Literature focus on major literary authors from Europe: Cervantes, Dante, Dostoyevsky, Goethe, Flaubert, Kafka, Pirandello and others. Some American texts might draw comparisons between these European authors and major American writers such as Faulkner or Hemingway. A Canadian volume would also refer to these canonical authors for comparisons, but would include texts by Canadian writers publishing in English or French such as Gabrielle Roy, Anne Hebert, Margaret Atwood, Robert Kroetsch, and Michael Ondaatje. In July, 2018, Ondaatje's novel *The English Patient* (1992) was awarded the Golden Man Booker Prize after being voted the best Booker winner in the past 50 years. The Canadian short-story writer, Alice Munro, won the Nobel Prize in Literature in 2013 and the Man Booker International Prize in 2009. Margaret Atwood won the Man Booker Prize in 2000 and many other international literary awards. There are many other Canadian authors such as M.G. Vassanji who have earned prizes and all this evidence makes plausible the argument for seeing Canadian works as having international value and for considering them suitable for comparative study in world literature. Many of these authors write with a significant awareness about foreign languages.

The Canadian approach to Comparative Literature would also include works by Indigenous authors such as Tomson Highway, Lee Maracle and Thomas King. Comparative study also allows us to explore ethnic minority authors in Canada who write in English, French and some heritage languages. This phenomenon of language diversity is not a practice that many American academics recognize or study.

In Canada we have established programs in Comparative Canadian Literature which have methodologies for reading ethnic minority writers. In the 1970s Comparative Canadian Literature study meant the examination of similarities between English Canadian texts and French Canadian texts. This approach was promulgated by Ronald Sutherland with *Second Image: Comparative Studies in Quebec/Canadian Literature* (1971). It became known as the Sherbrooke School of Comparative Canadian Literature. At the Université Laval, Clément Moisan published *Poésie des frontières: étude comparée des poésies canadienne et québécoise* (1979) which presented comparative studies from a French point of view and tended to harmonize with Sutherland's approach. At the Université de Montréal, Philip Stratford argued that comparative studies must also consider the differences as well as the similarities between

Québécois and Anglo-Canadian literatures. In 1979 Stratford was guest editor of an issue of the *Canadian Review of Comparative Literature* (6.2) devoted to Comparative Canadian Literature and which included contributions from several of the Canadian academics listed here. He also included work by women comparatists: Kathy Mezei, Eva-Marie Kroller and Patricia Merivale. Stratford reaffirmed his comparative arguments in his book, *All the Polarities* (1986).

The field began to expand in the 1980s to consider the study of ethnic-minority writers in Canada working in one of the two official languages but also a heritage language such as Italian, German, Ukrainian or Chinese. The model for this reading in diversity was provided by E.D. Blodgett with *Configuration: Essays on the Canadian Literatures* (1982). He further developed these arguments by including Indigenous authors in *Five-Part Invention: A History of Literary History in Canada* (2003).

By 1990 with the publication of *The Literatures of Lesser Diffusion/Les littératures de moindre diffusion* (Pivato) which collected essays on seventeen ethnic minority groups in Canada, it was well established that Comparative Literature had entered a new phase, which had yet to be acknowledged in the American academy.

This Canadian approach to Comparative Literature could be applied to the study of African literatures written in English, French and indigenous languages such as Swahili. It would give new approaches to colonial and post-colonial studies as demonstrated by the work of Ndeye Fatou Ba who is originally from Senegal but who now teaches in Canada (Ba).

Another important contribution that Comparative Literature made to Canada was the introduction of European feminist theory in French before it was translated into English and made available in the USA. The active person who brought together Quebec and English Canadian feminist writers was Barbara Godard, a comparatist and translator at York University in Toronto. She helped to create a network of women theorists.

Quebec writer and academic Madeline Gagnon taught for a time at the Université de Sherbrooke. In 1976 she co-authored with Hélène Cixous *La venue à l'écriture*. Cixous is the French feminist theorist who introduced the concept of *écriture féminine* in her 1975 essay, "Le rire de la Méduse" (The Laugh of the Medusa). Godard reviewed these publications in the feminist journal *Waves*, and later published "Language and Sexual Difference: the Case for Translation" (1984).

French theorist Julia Kristeva published her seminal book, *Sèméiotikè: recherches pour une sémanalyse*, in 1969. The English translation, *Desire in Language*, was published in 1980, long after the French text had been read by women writers in Quebec. The other psycholinguistic theorist besides Kristeva is Luce Irigaray whose two major works, *Speculum de l'autre femme* (1974) and *Ce sexe qui n'en est pas un* (1977), were read in Quebec, but did not appear in English in the United States until 1985. Quebec feminist Suzanne Lamay published *Marguerite Duras à Montréal* in 1981 after Quebec writers began to experiment with *le nouveau roman,* a narrative style that Duras helped to develop with her novel *Moderato Cantabile* (1958).

Barbara Godard co-founded the feminist literary theory journal *Tessera* in 1981-1982 with Daphne Marlatt, Kathy Mezei and Gail Scott. Quebec author Louise Cotnoir later joined the group of four editors. Louise Cotnoir and Gail Scott hosted regular Sunday meetings of women writers in Montreal and they often discussed feminist theory. One of the many bridges *Tessera* built was dialogue among women writers and academics in Quebec and English Canada.

Godard has an academic genealogy in Comparative Literature and theory. She earned an MA at the Université de Montréal under the supervision of Philip Stratford. In 1969 Godard completed a Maîtrise at the Université de Paris and in 1971 her PhD at the Université de Bordeaux; she taught for a time at the Université de Paris-Vincennes in the same department as Hélène Cixoux. Godard herself translated the work of key French-Canadian authors: Yolande Villemaire, France Théoret, Louky Bersianik, Nicole Brossard and Antonine Maillet. She promoted cross-linguistic discourse through her work in translation but also with academic articles in many literary journals and books such as *Collaboration in the Feminine: Writing on Women and Culture from Tessera* (1994).

Godard edited this book as a comparative collection that included essays by Québécois as well as ethnic minority women writers. In the introduction Godard lists some of the recurring topics that are now identified with comparative studies.

> Looking back on the body of work we eventually published, however, patterns emerge, a certain cohesion around issues such as the gendering of the critical institution in Canada, the crisis in representation, translation as a practice and an intellectual paradigm for border writing, gender and genre, narration especially, the question of the subject and the dominant symbolic order—a number of concerns now identified with post-structuralism and post-modernism. (Godard: 11)

There are two other feminist scholars who helped to bring comparative studies to Canadian literature. One of them is Patricia Smart who publishes her books in French and then self-translates them into English for a second publication. Her seminal book *Ecrire dans la maison du Père* (1988) became *Writing in the Father's House* (1991). The other is Christel Verduyn who edited the bilingual and multicultural collection *Literary Pluralities* (1998), which became a popular text in many literature courses across Canada. It is quite clear, even from this short survey of Canadian publications in Comparative Literature, that we have much to offer the world of comparative studies, despite being generally ignored by the American academy.

In this paper and in many other venues I have argued that Comparative Literature, at its core, is the study of texts in different languages (Pivato: 2018). But it is no longer just an exercise in language diversity. In 2020 Comparative Literature swings out beyond canonical text to study storytelling in other media such as film, opera and hypertext literature. A good example of this practice is Canadian comparatist Linda Hutcheon, who spent much of her career studying and teaching the postmodern novel in an international context. Later in her career she wrote about opera in a comparative approach that included medical history, in collaboration with her husband, Michael Hutcheon, a medical doctor. Their seminal text is *Opera: Desire, Disease, Death* (1996).

Despite these many success stories about Comparative Literature programs in Canada they are under attack from university administrations that do not support the study of languages and literatures beyond English and French. Comparative Literature programs and courses were closed at Vancouver's UBC in 2007. The Vice-President Academic tried to close the Comparative Literature Centre at the University of Toronto in 2010, but it was saved by an out-pouring of mail and petitions. The Comparative Literature program at the University of Alberta has been repeatedly restructured on its way to a slow and painful disappearance. In this dangerous environment we need books, scholars and readers that can argue for the value of Comparative Literature in Canada. The best argument for me is to actually produce a new Canadian book in Comparative Literature.

That book is *Comparative Literature for the New Century* (2018), which I co-edited with Giulia De Gasperi, and which is meant to promote the discipline of Comparative Literature by supporting the study of different languages. Most of the sixteen contributors are bilingual or trilingual Canadian scholars who argue for a truly multicultural approach to literary studies which are based on knowledge of the original languages of texts. The process of language exchange can be successful in the context of understanding cultural differences. This book has already stimulated a discussion on these issues: Susan Ingram and Irene Sywenky published a response, "X Marks the Spot: Literature and Theory as Limit Tests for Comparative Literature in the 21st Century, Canadian Perspectives," in the Spanish journal *452*F Revista de Teoria*.

We have a number of academic journals in Canada, such as *The Canadian Review of Comparative Literature* and *Mosaic*, that promote comparative study, but journals alone are not enough. We also need books which can be used as a classroom texts. Many things have changed in the comparative study of literature since the 1970s, but we still need to assert our existence in this important field of study by publishing books.

References

Ba, Ndwye Fatou. "Dialogue between Francophone and Anglophone Literatures in Africa." In De Gasperi and Pivato: 67-86.

Behdad, Ali & Dominic Thomas, eds. *A Companion to Comparative Literature*, Chichester, West Sussex and Malden, Massachusetts: Wiley-Blackwell, 2011.

Bernheimer, Charles. Ed. *Comparative Literature in the Age of Multiculturalism*. Baltimore and London: Johns Hopkins UP, 1995.

Blodgett, E.D. *Configuration: Essays on the Canadian Literatures*, ECW Press, 1982.

De Gasperi, Giulia, and Joseph Pivato, eds. *Comparative Literature for the New Century*, Montreal: McGill-Queen's U. P., 2018.

Dominguez, César, Haun Saussy & Dario Villanueva. *Introducing Comparative Literature: New Trends and Applications*. London: Routledge, 2015.

Foderaro, Lisa W. "Budget-Cutting Colleges Bid Some Languages Adieu." *The New York Times*, Dec. 3 (2010). Also available online.

Godard, Barbara. Ed. *Collaboration in the Feminine: Writings on Women and Culture from Tessera*. Toronto: Second Story Press, 1994.

_____. "Language and Sexual Difference: the Case of Translation." *Atkinson Review of Canadian Studies*, 2/1 (1984): 13-20.

Heise, Ursula K. Ed. *Futures of Comparative Literature: ACLA State of the Discipline Report*. London: Routledge, 2017.

Huston, Nancy. *Nord Perdu suivi de Douze France*. Arles: Actes Sud [coll. Babel], 1999.

Hutcheon, Linda. "Comparative Literature's 'Anxiogenic' State." *Canadian Review of Comparative Literature*, 23/1 (1996): 35-41.

_____. "Comparative Literature: Congenitally Contrarian." In Saussy: 224-229.

_____ and Michael Hutcheon. *Opera: Desire, Disease, Death*. Lincoln, Nebraska and London: University of Nebraska Press, 1996.

Ingram, Susan and Irene Sywenky. "X Marks the Spot: Literature and Theory as the Limit Tests for Comparative Literature in the 21st Century, Canadian Perspectives." *452*F Revista de Teoria de la Literatura y Literatura Comparada*, 20 (2019): 16-33.

Newman, Michael Z. "Intermediality and Transmedia Storytelling." The Centre for 21st Century Studies, University of Wisconsin-Milwaukee. Sept. 17, 2012. Retrieved August 20, 2018. www.c21uwm.com/2012/09/17/intermediality-and-transmedia-storytelling/

Pivato, Joseph. ed. *Literatures of Lesser Diffusion/Les littératures de moindre diffusion*. With the collaboration of S. Totosy de Zepetnek and M.V. Dimic. Edmonton: Research Institute for Comparative Literature, University of Alberta, 1990.

Pivato, Joseph. "The Languages of Comparative Literature." In De Gasperi and Pivato: 41-63.

Pratt, Mary Louise. "Comparative Literature and Global Citizenship." In Bernheimer: 58-65.

Saussy, Haun, ed. *Comparative Literature in an Age of Globalization*. Baltimore: Johns Hopkins UP, 2006.

Sieber, Tobin. "Sincerely Yours." In Bernheimer: 195-203.

Spivak, Gayatri Chakravorty. *Death of a Discipline*. New York: Columbia UP, 2003.

Stearns, Peter N. *Educating Global Citizens in Colleges and Universities: Challenges and Opportunities*. London: Routledge, 2008.

Stratford, Philip. *All the Polarities: Comparative Studies in Contemporary Canadian Novels in French and English*. Toronto: ECW Press, 1986.

Sutherland, Ronald. *Second Image: Comparative Studies in Quebec/Canadian Literature*. Toronto: New Press, 1971.

Part 2.
Making a Difference in Language, Literature and Literary Theory

Part 2

Nabokov's Languages

Alison Boulanger (Université de Lille)

Many of Nabokov's characters, like the author himself, come to know the discomforts of exile. Cut off from their place of birth, aloof from the one they inhabit, they strive to bridge the gap between countries and cultures, through the essential medium of language. In many of his writings, this results in interlinguistic word-play, and in two novels, in the creation of an alternate world where languages and literatures intermingle freely — Zembla in *Pale Fire* (1962) and Estotiland in *Ada or Ardor* (1969). The later novel, while exploring the lives and loves of Ada, Van and their half-sister Lucette, is placed in an imaginary world where geography and languages are recombined, so that the Northern part of the American continent, called Amerussia, and especially its province Estotiland, are peopled with English-, French- and Russian-speaking families. In this respect, Estotiland both strikingly mirrors, and strikingly diverges from, real Northern America. While the presence of "Canady French" mingling with an English-speaking population does in fact occur in parts of Canada, the presence of Russian peasantry and servants, and of a Russian aristocracy speaking Russian, English and French fluently, as well as German, emulates Nabokov's youthful surroundings or, alternately, conflates the various countries he successively inhabited: Russia in his youth, then England, Germany and France through the 1920s and 1930s, followed by the United States to which he escaped in the face of inexorable Nazi advance. It is tempting to read *Ada* as countering the solitude of the emigrant: while the author may have felt like a linguistic anomaly in the various stages of his exile, he invented for his characters a world where Russian existed on an equal footing with English, and could be freely interspersed with French and, to a lesser degree, German or other languages.

By contrast, Kinbote, the protagonist of *Pale Fire*, is a markedly isolated figure, socially, sexually and linguistically, both unable and unwilling to fit in the American university town where he has taken refuge from the political turmoil of his native country, Zembla. In this novel, Nabokov, not content with inventing a new country, invented a language for it. This makes *Pale Fire* unusual even by comparison with other Nabokovian works. Though many if not all of his novels have plurilingual protagonists, who delight in plurilingual wordplay, in *Pale Fire* the question of languages, their idiosyncrasies and their inter-relatedness, is an even more central concern. Not only does Kinbote constantly harp on problems of expression and translation, but his self-appointed task is to edit and comment a poem, also entitled "Pale Fire," written by the recently-deceased American poet John Shade. The 999 lines of Shade's poem form the central part of the work, framed with Kinbote's introduction, notes and index; and as in this poem, Shade frequently voices his thoughts about language(s), they enter in a dialogue of sorts with Kinbote's on Zemblan, Russian, English, French and other idioms.

While *Pale Fire* has attracted a great deal of critical attention, the uniqueness of Zemblan as linguistic melting-pot has rarely been the focus-point. Critics have not been blind to the issues of exile, plurilingual abilities, or translation, so that Zemblan has usually been studied in the light of one or all of these questions, rather than in itself. While I am aware that in studying an imaginary idiom I am trespassing on the grounds of Star Trek fandom or Tolkien specialists, I would like to take a closer look at this one, so for the purposes of this paper, I shall set the plot aside (thrilling as it is), in order to focus on this unusual web of languages.

1. Creative (mis)translation

Like counterparts from other Nabokovian novels, the characters in *Pale Fire* love to play with words, one of their games being word-golf, e.g. going from "hate" to "love" in three strikes.[1] They also enjoy the surprise which comes from reversing certain words, "spider" turning into "redips," "powder" in "red wop," and poor "T.S. Eliot" into the laborious "toilest" (note to lines 347-348: 154). And like Hermann Karlovitch, Humbert Humbert, Vadim Vadimitch, Ada, Van or others, they seem particularly fond of conflating two or more languages in fertile word-play, as Shade does at the beginning of Canto Three:

> *L'if*, lifeless tree! Your great Maybe, Rabelais:
> The grand potato. (Lines 501-2: 44)

The first word, *L'if*, apostrophizes a tree, the yew, by its French name and article; it is followed by "lifeless tree" which highlights the funeral associations of the yew (as an evergreen, it is very much in favour in cemeteries as well as topiary), but also, paradoxically, the graphic proximity of the French *L'if* and the English "life." *L'if* also calls to mind, implicitly, its homograph, the English conjunction "if," denoting uncertainty, which while not physically present ushers in "maybe." This word, in its turn, calls on a French equivalent, *peut-être*, which like "*if*/if" combines the idea of uncertainty and the reference to death since Rabelais (as Kinbote explains in note to line 502: 176) is rumoured to have said on his deathbed "*Je m'en vais chercher le grand peut-être*." But this "*grand peut-être*" is in turn comically deflated and brought back to a homely vegetable, "the grand potato." Kinbote, in his note, deprecates this "execrable pun," while he approves of another instance of interlingual word-play where Shade, in one of the discarded variants of his poem, translates his name into the French *ombre* and then, implicitly, into the Spanish *hombre* (see note to line 275: 139: "I like my name: Shade, *Ombre*, almost 'man'/In Spanish")–at least if Kinbote is to be relied upon for a faithful

---

[1] This and other examples are given in note to line 819, p. 206, in Vladimir Nabokov, *Pale Fire* [1962], Harmondsworth (Middlesex), Penguin Books, 1973. All quotes are from this edition and page references will be supplied parenthetically; I shall also indicate lines when quoting from Shade's poem, or from Kinbote's notes.

transcription of the draft. In another passage of the poem proper, Shade remembers

> That Englishman in Nice,
> A proud and happy linguist: *je nourris*
> *Les pauvres cigales*—meaning that he
> Fed the poor sea gulls!
> Lafontaine was wrong:
> Dead is the mandible, alive the song. (Lines 240-245: 36)

Here, too, the Englishman's error introduces a playful collusion of *cigales* (cicada) and sea-gulls, so that the birds recall the care-free but ultimately famished insect of La Fontaine's fable.

Besides combining various real languages in fertile interplay, *Pale Fire* introduces an imaginary language, Zemblan, which is itself a combination of Nabokov's beloved Russian with various other European languages (mostly those which exhibit markedly Northern and Germanic traits). Thus, when Kinbote quotes a Zemblan poem,

> On ságaren werém tremkín tri stána
> Verbálala wod gev ut trí phantána (note to line 80: 89)

—a poem which he kindly translates for his readers, "a dream king in the sandy wastes of time would give three hundred camels and three fountains" (*ibid.*)—Indo-European roots clearly appear through their thin Zemblan veneer: *tremkin*, or dream king, is reminiscent of the German *Traum König*, *ut* may combine the German *und* and the French *et*... Some words are more transparently English (*wod gev* for *would give*), some are close to both Russian and English (*tri phantana*, three fountains). The imaginary language seems to bring English closer to Germanic and Russian counterparts, and occasionally to other languages.

Zemblan thus creates a sort of meeting ground for world-languages and world-literature. Kinbote, for instance, discusses various translations made by John Shade (whom Kinbote worships) and his wife Sybil (whom Kinbote criticizes out of evident jealousy), and always attempts his own translation into Zemblan. When Shade echoes Goethe's "*Erlenkönig*" in a passage of his poem, "Who rides so late in the night and the wind? / It is the writer's grief. It is the wild / March wind. It is the father with his child" (lines 662-664: 48), Kinbote comments:

> One cannot sufficiently admire the ingenious way in which Shade manages to transfer something of the broken rhythm of the ballad (a trisyllabic meter at heart) into his iambic verse:
> 662 Who rídes so láte in the níght and the wínd
> [...]
> 664 [...] Ít is the fáther wíth his child
> Goethe's two lines opening the poem come out most exactly and beautifully, with the bonus of an unexpected rhyme (also in French: *vent-enfant*), in my own language:
> Ret wóren ok spóz on nátt ut vétt?
> Éto est vótchez ut míd ik détt.

As is often the case when Kinbote quotes Zemblan, the language seems to incorporate Russian words or phrases, e.g. "*Eto est votchez*" (with recognizable Indo-Europan roots), and more Germanic ones, e.g. "*mıd*" for "*mit*," or "*natt ut vett*," which might equally echo Russian or the German "*Nacht und Wind*." Zemblan is thus at the cross-roads of European languages and literatures, just as Goethe's poem is, since Goethe drew on his friend Herder's translations from Danish poetry when writing "*Erlenkönig*." The very title is indebted to the process of translation and its mishaps, since Herder mistakenly translated the Danish "*Ellerkong*" (or king of the elves) as "*Erlenkönig*" (or king of the alder trees)–a felicitous, if unintentional, type of plurilingual word-play, such as Nabokovian characters delight in. Goethe's poem thus appears as a link in a long chain of plurilingual rewritings, from Danish original to Herderian (mis)translation to Goethean rewriting, which in turn inspires further translators and writers such as Shade or Kinbote (to say nothing of composers). So that while Kinbote is an extremely unlikable character, unscrupulous editor and unreliable narrator, he nonetheless voices crucial tenets of Nabokov's aesthetics, especially on the subject of language and literature, envisioned as translational processes through space and time.

2. At the roots of English language and literature?

The emphasis Nabokov places on rewriting and translation in *Pale Fire* has led a critic, Priscilla Meyer (1988), to surmise that the novel consciously rewrites a number of works: religious poems written by, or under the patronage of, King Alfred the Great (at the end of the 9th century); the Icelandic *Eddas*;[2] the anonymous Russian epic *Song of Igor's Campaign*; the *Songs of Ossian* by James MacPherson (18th century), and Elias Lönrot's *Kalevala* (1835). The fact that one of these works (MacPherson's) was a fabrication, and another (the *Song of Igor's Campaign*) was long suspected of being one, does not require discussion here; more to the point, these are works which, by garnering various narratives, strive to save them from oblivion and relay them to future generations. MacPherson thus created a fictitious Celtic bard, Ossian, in order to preserve ancient poetic forms, and Elias Lönrot set out to preserve the lore of Finland — much as Snorri Sturluson (in earlier times) had preserved and exemplified forms of skaldic poetry in his *Edda*. Those works, therefore, have come to embody languages and cultures which might otherwise have disappeared. By the same token, if Alfred the Great plays a part in *Pale Fire*, it might be not so much because, like the fictitious king of Zembla, he was forced into flight by dangerous foreign invaders, living in disguise and (in a manner of speaking) in exile, but because once restored to a position of power he devoted much of his life to collecting works, and to translating and writing in West-Saxon, thus playing a major part in the development of English language and literature.

If Priscilla Meyer is right in contending that these works play a central part in *Pale Fire*, then the novel aims at no less than going back to the very sources of European, and especially English, literature. Her central thesis is, in fact, that in drawing on such a body of works, Nabokov was emphasizing the part played by Anglo-Saxon and Scandinavian voyagers in the development of the

---

[2] That is, the "Elder" or "Poetic" *Edda*, an anonymous collection of some twenty epics probably going back to the 10th and 11th century, but which resurfaced later than the "Younger" or "Prose" *Edda*, composed by Snorri Sturluson (1179-1241).

English language and literature. The language, of course, was decisively shaped by successive waves of Northern invaders with Germanic idioms, Angles, Saxons and Jutes followed by Danes, Norwegian and Swedes, all leaving their mark on place-names and customs, on language and literature, only to be displaced by Norman custom and idiom. Since some of these fearless Northern explorers travelled far into Russia, where they also left their mark, Meyer feels that in drawing attention to them, Nabokov was linking present English not only to its Northern and Germanic past, but to his own Russian past.

As attractive as this theory seems, it must be pointed out that Meyer's work has met with sceptical reactions amongst Nabokov critics, Brian Boyd for one.[3] In truth, a reader going through *Pale Fire* will find little to support her thesis that the religious poems of Alfred the Great or the *Songs of Ossian* play such a significant part. While there are allusions to those works, as well as to the *Kalevala* or the *Eddas*, any of Nabokov's novels will provide a cluster of allusions to any number of literary, pictural and/or musical works, and nothing seems to justify the central position that Meyer claims for these specific works. And while her learned analysis is convincing in some of the intertextual links it uncovers, her general thesis appears to over-interpret scarce and scattered allusions into a seemingly cogent, but ultimately baseless theory, much as Kinbote himself over-interprets John Shade's poem to the point of creating an alternate version. Appreciation of Meyer's method may, indeed, depend on the light in which Kinbote himself is seen, as a fanatic who refuses to recognize any reading other than his own (flawed as it is), or as a rewriter who appropriates Shade's material into his own creative process. And this in turn depends on the light in which literary criticism, and the literary text itself, are seen: if there is no text *per se*, if a text is only a sort of free-for-all, the sum

---

[3] "In her extremely erratic *Find What the Sailor has Hidden* […], Priscilla Meyer provides many attempted glosses to the novel in pursuit of a dotty thesis that '*Pale Fire* effects a synthesis of British and American culture, outlining the thousand-year evolution of the Anglo-American tradition from the end of the reign of King Alfred in 899 to the birth of Vladimir Vladimirovich in 1899,'" Boyd: 269, endnote 9.

of its infinite readings (as Rorty, for one, contends), then all readings are allowable and none can be rejected as irrelevant. If, on the other hand, a text may be apprehended independently of its critical readings, then these may be measured and, occasionally, found wanting.[4]

Given the central role which interpretation plays in Nabokov's *Pale Fire*, it is not surprising that the novel should fuel such fierce critical debates. But while her book raises many questions, Meyer may be given credit for pointing out Nabokov's keen awareness of, and pleasure in, relating languages and cultures to one another. Mad as he seems to be, Kinbote consistently draws attention to the circulation and inter-relatedness of literatures and languages. Thus he draws a parallel between a discarded line in Shade's drafts and "a charming quatrain from our Zemblan counterpart of the Elder Edda, in an anonymous English translation (Kirby's?) […]" (note to line 79: 88). Of course, this is typical of Kinbote, bringing the spotlight back on Zembla at every turn, but it is also typical of Nabokov's views on literature, with the Edda fostering a Zemblan counterpart, which generates an English translation, which in turn inspires an American poet. As with Goethe's poem, and indeed countless instances throughout *Pale Fire*, literature circulates and disseminates, linking old and new, intermingling languages and cultures, and playing an instrumental part in their development. And while the *Eddas* might not play quite as crucial a part as Meyer contends, Kinbote's imaginary Zembla does, indeed, function as a northern arc linking Germanic (and by implication English) languages and literatures to Russian—with a smattering of Latin and other languages for flavour.

While Nabokov is careful not to locate Zembla too precisely, it is clear that it occupies a strategic position, in a Northern part of Europe, and in close proximity to (Soviet) Russia. (The very name Zembla points the reader northwards, since it echoes that of a real island, Novaya Zemlya, which is to be found between the Barents and Kara seas.) Geographically and politically, Zembla alternately

---

[4] See the debate between Umberto Eco and Richard Rorty in Eco, Rorty, Culler and Brooke-Rose (1992).

functions as meeting-ground, buffer zone and/or battle ground between Russia and other areas. From a linguistic point of view, too, it occupies an intermediary position, since Zemblan exhibits both Slavic and Germanic roots. Kinbote casually scatters Slav-sounding words like "*vebodar* (upland pastures)" (note to line 137: 111) or "*moskovett*, that bitter blast" (note to line 230: 134), along with more politically and historically charged words (*komizars*, note to line 130: 97, or *shpiks* to denote plainclothes-policemen, note to line 149: 119); he adds a sprinkling of potentially Latin words like *coramen* (note to line 137: 111), or the suffix *-ula* in "*situla* (toy pail)" (note to line 130: 101). But Germanic or Anglo-Saxon composite words are no less obvious, such as "*kamergrum* (groom of the chamber)" (note to line 80: 90) or "*lumbarkamer*" (note to line 130: 109), which combines Germanicized versions of "lumber" and "chamber."

More than once, Zemblan does seem to mirror the composite origins of English. Kinbote mentions a Zemblan character named Shalksbore, a name he translates as "knave's farm" (note to lines 433-434: 166), stating that it is "the most probable derivation of "Shakespeare" (*ibid.*): thus the quintessential English playwright and poet suddenly grows Scandinavian roots. No less unexpectedly, Norman-French ramifications follow, for this same Shalksbore is nicknamed Curdy Buff (*ibid.*), an anglicized version of Cœur-de-Bœuf. This name, which Nabokov obviously invests with sexual meaning,[5] strongly suggests Norman ancestry (according to etymologists, the family names and place names ending in "bœuf," which abound in Normandy, are to be traced back to Scandinavian origins). The Zemblan character's name and nickname echo the process by which English literature, and the English language, have been shaped by successive waves of Anglo-Saxon, Danish and Norman invaders. Similar associations cluster around the maiden-name of John Shade's wife, Sybil Irondell, for Kinbote is careful to warn his readers that this name "comes not

---

[5] In *Ada*, Van's rival Percy de Prey, urinating in a stream, exhibits his "engine, surgically circumcised, terrifically oversized and high-coloured, with such a phenomenal *cœur de bœuf* [...]," in Part One, chapter 39: 217. By analogy with the shape of a bovine's heart, the "*cœur de bœuf*" here is probably Percy's glans.

from a little valley yielding iron ore but from the French for 'swallow'" (note to line 247: 138). Once more, English-speaking readers face the composite origins of their language: where they might have identified recognizable English words ("shake spear," "iron dell") with Germanic roots, Kinbote's explanations usher in Norman origins, reminiscent of the Arundell, companions to William the Conqueror who settled in Cornwall. From then on, Kinbote keeps playing with the name of Shade's wife, dubbing her "Sybil Swallow" for instance (see note to line 275: 139). While such wordplay is above all an expression of Kinbote's spiteful resentment towards Sybil (whom he perceives as an unworthy rival for Shade's favour, and whom he is accordingly reluctant to call "Mrs Shade"), it makes her name flit to-and-fro across the Channel, mimicking the interplay of Old French and Old English at the court of Norman and, later, Plantagenet rulers. And since "swallow" in English can be either a noun for a migrating bird or a verb for the act of ingesting, Meyer may well be right in viewing this as a specific reference to one of the first myths referred to both in the Elder, or Poetic *Edda*, and in Snorri Sturluson's Younger or Prose *Edda*:

> A certain giantess lives [...] in a forest called Ironwood. [...] The ancient giantess breeds as sons many giants and all in wolf shapes [...]. And they say that from this clan will come a most mighty one called Moongarm. He [...] will swallow heavenly bodies and spatter heaven and all the skies with blood. Thus it says in *Voluspa*:
> In the east lives the old one, in Ironwood, and breeds there Fenrir's kind. Out of them all comes one in particular, sun's snatcher in troll's guise. (Snorri Sturluson: 15)

Kinbote's harping on the words "Sybil," "iron dell" and "swallow" might be, as Meyer surmises, a disguised allusion to this Icelandic myth, told by a kind of sybil (the title *Voluspa*, the part of the *Elder Edda* where this tale is told, means "prophecy of the seeress"), predicting the demise of the sun, swallowed by a wolf born in Ironwood.

But even a reader who misses this erudite point will probably be struck at the many possible readings of the words "Irondell" and "swallow," according to whether they are traced back to a

Germanic or a Norman-French origin, to a former invasion or to a later. Kinbote makes much the same point as the jester Wamba at the beginning of Scott's *Ivanhoe*, showing that invasion and settlement (however traumatic in themselves) lead to a rich if asymmetrical interplay of idioms, multi-layered, strongly hierarchized, yet dynamic. Once more, the seeming unity of English is a mere surface, under which careful readers are invited to decipher complex historical, sociopolitical and linguistic developments. To borrow a phrase of Deleuze and Guattari, the Nabokovian reader is expected to undergo a voluntary process of deterritorialization and inhabit his or her own language like a foreigner.[6]

From Herder, Goethe, and their younger Romantic counterparts down to Nabokov, Rainer Maria Rilke or Samuel Beckett, one may trace a long line of authors who, by compulsion or by choice, learned more than one language, and came to express the belief that such plurilingualism was essential to writing; that the clash of different idioms would force writers out of their unthinking, daily use of language, making them compare systems, uncover fruitful similarities and even more fruitful differences, discover the foreign roots of familiar words. Nabokov's aim is clearly to make his readers see their own language anew, enhancing its aesthetic potential. Perhaps no less crucially, the protagonists' plurilingualism, and the author's, will appear far less unusual if readers are brought to the realization that no language is ever actually "single." By unearthing the variegated origins of English and its development over time, Nabokov enmeshes his own creative processes in the rich and complex flow of European languages and literatures.

Zemblan may appear as a highly artificial language to many an irritated reader, but in point of fact it reminds English-speaking readers of the Germanic roots of their language; under their weird Zemblan disguise, familiar words are linked to their distant Anglo-Saxon, Scandinavian or Norman origins. Thus Zemblan allows

---

6   "Être dans sa propre langue comme un étranger […]," Deleuze and Guattari: 64.

Nabokov to scrutinize the English language, to uncover its buried past, to emphasize its multiplicity under the seeming unity of its surface, to make strangeness appear where all seemed reassuringly familiar. This is definitely a central tenet of Nabokovian poetics: while taking a language for granted makes it sink in the meaningless commonplace,[7] the philological and poetical approach combine to rattle the readers out of their assumptions. In this respect, *Pale Fire*, a comparatist's paradise, functions as a compendium of world-literature, a fertile method for grafting languages onto one another, an exercise in de-familiarization within a familiar language. What seems well-known thus reveals new depths, and meaning is always on the move.

References

Primary sources

Nabokov, Vladimir. *Pale Fire* (1962). Harmondsworth (Middlesex): Penguin Books, 1973.

Nabokov, Vladimir. *Ada* (1969). Harmondsworth (Middlesex): Penguin Books, 1970.

Nabokov, Vladimir. *Strong Opinions*. New York: Random House (Vintage Books), 1990.

Sturluson, Snorri. *Edda*. Transl. and ed. by Anthony Faulkes. London: J.M. Dent ["Everyman"], 1987.

Critical References

Boyd, Brian. *Nabokov's Pale Fire: The Magic of Artistic Discovery*. Princeton (N.J.) and Oxford: Princeton University Press, 1999.

Eco, Umberto. "Overinterpreting texts" and "Reply" [to Rorty's paper]. In Umberto Eco, Richard Rorty, Jonathan Culler and Christine Brooke-Rose. *Interpretation and Overinterpretation*, ed. by Stefan Collini. Cambridge: Cambridge University Press, 1992: 45-66 and 139-151.

---

[7] "To be sure, there is an average reality, perceived by all of us, but that is not true reality: it is only the reality of general ideas, conventional forms of humdrummery, current editorials. [...] Average reality begins to rot and stink as soon as the act of individual creation ceases to animate a subjectively perceived texture," Nabokov, *Strong Opinions*: 118.

Deleuze, Gilles and Félix Guattari. *Kafka. Pour une littérature mineure.* Paris: Minuit, 1975.

Meyer, Priscilla. *Find What the Sailor Has Hidden: Vladimir Nabokov's Pale Fire.* Middletown (Connecticut): Wesleyan University Press, 1988.

Rorty, Richard. "The Pragmatist's Progress." In Eco, Rorty, Culler and Brooke-Rose. *Interpretation and Overinterpretation*: 89-108.

Proust's and Woolf's Dialogue Regarding Language

Tamar Barbakadze (UNIL)

Virginia Woolf read and admired Marcel Proust. Her letters to Roger Eliot Fry, diary, essays and novels record her admiration. Apart from being an attentive reader of the French writer, Woolf herself played an important role in Proust's reception in the Anglo-Saxon world. From as early as the 1920s, her writings, be they *intermediary*, i.e., the diaries, the letters, the autobiographical writings, or her *oeuvre*, started to inform the English readers about Proust's work. The importance she awarded to Proust's work figures prominently in her essays, namely in "The Novels of E. M. Forster" (1927), "On Not Knowing Greek" (1925) and "Robinson Crusoe" (1926). In the essay "Robinson Crusoe," Woolf labels Proust as the "great writer" in whose "masterpiece [...] the vision is clear and order has been achieved" (*Common Reader*, henceforth CR: 54). Woolf also includes Proust in her palimpsest *A Room of One's Own* (1929) under the list of androgynous authors next to Shakespeare and Jane Austen, who could write from the combination of masculine and feminine perspectives.

Woolf wished to write like Proust. She wrote to Roger Fry: "Oh if I could write like that!" (*Letters*, II: 525), namely like Proust. It has been said that the French writer "must have very greatly influenced her work" (Hoare, 1938: 43). Woolf indeed shares aesthetic sensibility and themes, such as concepts of time and memory, with Proust. Yet, some thematic affinities between *À la recherche du temps perdu* and Woolf's works must be simply coincidental. Both suggest that words were used differently in the period of the First World War. Woolf reacts against the abuse of language in her two polemics *A Room of One's Own* and *Three Guineas* (1938) and in her novel *To the Lighthouse* (1927), to name a few. In his last volume, *Le temps retrouvé (Time Regained)*, Proust also appears as a critic of the misuse of the power of language in the context of World War 1. By the time Virginia Woolf published *To the Lighthouse* and *A Room of One's Own* she had already read Proust's volumes namely *Du côté de chez Swann* and *À l'ombre des jeunes filles en fleur*.[1] Despite her acquaintance with *La Recherche*, she could not have been influenced in all areas of production by Proust's work. This article shows that Proust and Woolf react against the misuse of the power of language in support of violence. Even if there is a similarity between the two novelists' ideas, we can see the differences which lie in the aesthetic strategies they adopted in opposition to the propagandistic use of language.

Proust and Woolf take up the problem of language in the context of World War 1. War-time, for Proust, puts language in danger as much as the reality of the front is unspeakable. The battlefields "seemed to [civilians] unreal merely because it was only through the papers [they] had heard of [combatants] and [the civilians] could not realise [that the combatants] had been taking part in Titanic combats and had come back with only a bruise on the shoulder" (*Time Regained*: 49).[2] The papers use language as a tool to persuade the audience by confounding the ordinary meaning of words; whereas Saint-Loup's return from the front is as difficult to represent as a return from hell, from the "shores of death" (*ibid.*), as Proust himself puts it.[3] The reality of the war is beyond imagination and cannot be put into words. Quite the

---

[1] The English began to read Proust's last volume in their mother tongue from the year 1930 onwards, when Charles Kenneth Scott Moncrieff translated it (Philippe, 2016: 6). Woolf had read Proust's first volume *Swann's Way* in the original by May 1922 (*Letters*, II, p. 525), i.e., a few months earlier than it was translated in English. She could have read Proust in English since September 1922, when C.K. Scott Moncrieff translated the first volume *Du côté de chez Swann*. By 1925 Woolf had read Proust's two volumes, *Swann's Way* and *Within a Budding Grove*, as she explains in her letter to Margaret Llewelyn Davies, February 9, 1925 (*Letters*, III: 166).

[2] All references to *Time Regained* are to Stephen Hudson's translation, London, Chatto & Windus, 1931, available online: http://gutenberg.net.au. For the original text see: "Et en effet ils ne venaient pas seulement de lieux qui nous semblaient irréels parce que nous n'en avions entendu parler que par les journaux et que nous ne pouvions nous figurer qu'on eût pris part à ces combats titaniques et revenir avec seulement une contusion à l'épaule," *Le Temps retrouvé* : 617.

[3] "[...] des rivages de la mort," *ibid.*

opposite, "it is extraordinary, in those who have been resurrected from the front [...], that the only effect of this contact with the mystery is to increase, were that possible, the insignificance of our intercourse with them" (*ibid.*).[4] In the war-time, "a few simple words," Proust stated, "were little different from what they would have been before the war" (*Time Regained*: 49). Yet, old words were applied to unusual significations: "the tone of intercourse remain[ed] the same, the matter differ[ed]" (*ibid.*).[5] Proust expresses his surprise that words remained the same when the experiences of the war clearly altered people's view of the world. "Words no longer do anything" (*Time Regained*: 46).[6] For instance, "the word 'poilu' has become [...] something which [...] can no more [be] regard[ed] as implying an allusion or a joke" (*ibid.*).[7] Words like *poilu*, according to Proust, are "awaiting great poets like such words as 'Deluge' or 'Christ' or 'Barbarians' which were saturated with grandeur before Hugo, Vigny and the rest used them" (*ibid.*).[8] Proust suggests that, on the one hand, words often corrupt in the context of the war and do not evoke the meaning they are supposed to; on the other hand, the experiences of the front are beyond expression. A few years later, Woolf also noted that words lost their value in the course of the war (*AROO*: 12). The war has had its impact on the sound and ultimately, on the meaning and value of the words. Woolf highlighted: "before the war [...] the same things

---

[4] "Car il est extraordinaire à quel point chez les rescapés du feu que sont les permissionnaires [...] le seul effet du contact avec le mystère soit d'accroître, s'il est possible, l'insignifiance des propos," *ibid*.

[5] "[...] il ne m'avait dit que de simples paroles. Encore étaient-elles fort peu différentes de ce qu'elles eussent été avant la guerre, comme si les gens, malgré elle, continuaient à être ce qu'ils étaient; le ton des entretiens était le même, la matière seule différait," *ibid*.

[6] "L'épopée est tellement belle que tu trouverais comme moi que les mots ne font plus rien," as Saint-Loup writes in a letter, *Le Temps retrouvé*: 614.

[7] Again, from Saint-Loup's letter (*ibid.*); "poilu" means a French soldier in the First World War (*Le Robert* online).

[8] "Au contact d'une telle grandeur, le mot 'poilu' est devenu pour moi quelque chose dont je ne sens même pas plus s'il a pu contenir d'abord une allusion ou une plaisanterie que quand nous lisons 'chouans' par exemple. Mais je sens 'poilu' déjà prêt pour de grands poètes, comme les mot déluge, ou Christ, ou Barbares qui étaient déjà pétris de grandeur avant que s'en fussent servis Hugo, Vigny, ou les autres," again from Saint-Loup's letter, *Le Temps retrouvé*: 614.

[...] would have sounded different" (*ibid.*) In the pre-war years, "people would have said precisely the same things," but "in those days [words] were accompanied by a sort of humming noise, not articulate, but musical" (*ibid.*). Woolf thus suggests that the war altered the balance between the words' sound and value.

Why do Proust and Woolf suggest the sweep of language in the context of the First World War? What political depth may we recognize in their own practices with language? In response to these questions this article includes the analysis of certain passages from Woolf's and Proust's texts. Woolf's critical perspectives regarding language and her own lexical resistance to representing the war catastrophes in their immediacy are made available in her essays *A Room of One's Own* and *Three Guineas* and in the middle section of *To the Lighthouse*, respectively. The essays allow us to see how the "strange [...] diabolic power which words possess" (*Selected Essays*, henceforth *SE*: 88) is exercised in support of the Great War. We will also notice that the middle panel of *To the Lighthouse*, "Time Passes," represents the brutality of the war through figurative language. Proust also expresses his views about the problem of language in the final volume of *La Recherche*, *Le Temps retrouvé* (in English *Time Regained*), which develops around Paris during the First World War, i.e., between 1914 and 1918. Like Woolf, Proust describes the war far away from the killing fields.

In "Time Passes" and *Le Temps retrouvé*, war gets reflected without the reader being prepared for it. The war breaks the story in both works. It arrives very unexpectedly in Proust's last volume, just as it does in *To the Lighthouse*. The middle section "Time Passes," which is commonly known to encompass ten years, connects pre-war and post-war times. Woolf described the structure of *To the Lighthouse* as "two blocks joined by a corridor."[9] The corridor defines "Time Passes" (part 2). It connects two single days presented in the first and last parts of the novel. The images in the "Window" section (part 1) evoke the pre-war years of unity that Mrs. Ramsay ensured, and the lighthouse symbolized. Part 3 of the book, "The Lighthouse," no longer provides the primary order,

---

[9] *To the Lighthouse: The Original Holograph Draft*, 1982 (henceforth *OHD*): 48.

because the mother, Mrs. Ramsay, is no longer alive. Two of the Ramsays' children are also missing: Andrew has been killed in the war and Prue has died in childbirth. A "merging and flowing" (*To the Lighthouse*, henceforth *TL*: 95) atmosphere in the Ramsays' house is replaced by the metaphors of the war such as "advance guards of great armies" (*TL*: 147) that "enter [...] the drawing-room, questioning and wondering" (*TL*: 144). The metaphor of fertilization—reflecting Mrs. Ramsay's artistry at arranging the dinner table—is followed by the metaphors of ruin and decay. On the pages of "The Window," Mrs Ramsay serves the "Bœuf en Daube," which took the cook three days to prepare (*TL*: 120), and "a yellow and purple dish of fruit" including "the grapes and pears, [...] the horny pink-lined shell, [...] the bananas" reminding her "of a trophy fetched from the bottom of the sea, of Neptune's banquet, of the bunch that hangs with vine leaves over the shoulder of Bacchus" (*TL*: 110)—the mythical god of wine-harvest and fertility.[10] By contrast, in Part 2, "the fertility, the insensibility of nature" take over the Ramsays' vacant house (*TL*: 158). The looking-glass on the wall no longer holds a human "face," "a figure," a "hand" or "children" who would "come in rushing and tumbling" (*TL*: 147). It reflects "only the shadows of the trees, flourishing in the wind" (*TL*: 141) and other "form[s] from which life had parted" (*TL*: 147-148). In the dehumanized world of "Time Passes," darkness and "nothingness" (*TL*: 143-145) fill the Ramsays' summer house. "Certain airs, detached from the body of the wind," seem to "venture indoors" (*TL*: 144). If in Part 1, the house is "filled with [humans'] words" (*TL*: 43), in Part 2, "a giant voice shriek(s) loud in its agony" (*TL*: 152).

The immediacy of war is also found in *Le Temps retrouvé*. Proust's metaphors of floral fertilization, the poetical language and floral aesthetics get suddenly replaced by military metaphors: "jewels evoking the armies by their decorative theme" (*Time Regained*: 26).[11] Fashion trends bring the war to mind. For instance,

---

[10] See "Dionysus God Of—Greek Mythology," www.theoi.com
[11] "de bijoux évoquant les armées par leur thème décoratif," *Le Temps retrouvé*: 591-592.

"young women [...] w[ea]r straight Egyptian tunics, dark and very 'warlike' above their short skirts" and "high leggings like those of our beloved combatants" (*ibid*.).[12] Exhibitions in Paris are no longer devoted to the work of artists "admired till then" (*ibid*.) but to clothing.[13] While "the Louvre and all the museums were closed" (*ibid*.: 27), the dressmakers rather than artists sought to discover "a new formula of beauty for the generations after the war" (*ibid*.).[14] Thus, Proust places more emphasis on man's changing vision and tendency to replace the refined art form by the war-inspired dresses than on describing Paris at war.

Some of Woolf's critics, such as Zwerdling, Haule, Levenback and Tratner, suggest that the "Time Passes" section primarily focuses on the First World War, even if *To the Lighthouse* may not be recognized as a war novel. Indeed, a sudden passage from human perception and language (part 1) to the world of chaos and catastrophes, outside consciousness and logic (part 2), invites interpretation of Woolf's novel in light of the historical context. If Part 1 is concerned with the human viewers and the humans viewed, the middle panel does not describe the world through the human perspective and the war in its immediate expression. The characters' shifting points of view available in Part 1 are replaced by the "gigantic chaos" (*TL*: 154) in Part 2. "With the lamps all put out" (*TL*: 143), the world has become "eyeless" (*TL*: 154), i.e., with disabled eyes, if not completely blind. Various war metaphors further contribute to acknowledge World War 1 as the main scale of reference in the "Time Passes" section.[15] For instance, "the universe [...] battling and tumbling in brute confusion" (*TL*: 154), "idiot games" (*ibid*.), "flesh turned to atoms" (*TL*: 126), among many, allude to the killing fields of the Great War.

---

12 "des jeunes femmes [...] ayant des tuniques égyptiennes droites, sombres, très 'guerre,' sur des jupes très courtes ; elles chaussaient [...] de hautes guêtres rappelant celles de nos chers combattants," *ibid*.: 591.
13 "admiré jusque-là," *ibid*.: 593.
14 "Le Louvre, tous les musées étaient fermés [...]," "dégager pour les générations d'après la guerre une formule nouvelle du beau [...]," *ibid*.: 592.
15 For military metaphors in "Time Passes" see my article "Catherine Colomb et Virginia Woolf. 'Raconter' la guerre à travers des métaphores," 2021: 163-176.

In Woolf's world, the words keep the memory of the war. The examples of how the war reversed the meaning of words are given in *To the Lighthouse*. As the novel progresses the words "full," "house" and "lighthouse" take on new meanings. In the "Window" section, "the house seemed full of children sleeping and Mrs Ramsay listening; shaded lights and regular breathing" (*TL*: 56). In "Time Passes," Woolf repeats the phrase "(the house was full again)" (*TL*: 162) within the parenthesis. However, the group of words contains altered meaning in its recurrence. The phrases "The house seemed full" and "the house was full again" do not contain the same meaning at all. Rather the word "full" acquires opposite meanings in different contexts. In the first sentence (in Part 1), the word "full" implies that Mrs. Ramsay and her children live in the house, whereas in the second sentence (in Part 2), it means that the Ramsays' house is vacant. Likewise, the word "house" refers to the Ramsays' residence on the Isle of Skye in Part 1 of the novel. In the middle part its meaning extends to the size of the whole earth. The Ramsays' house becomes a metaphor of "the white earth" (*TL*: 151). The reader may also recognize the changed perspective of the key word "lighthouse." James's childhood dream of reaching the lighthouse later transforms into the motif of a homeward journey of personal change rooted in *The Odyssey*. Woolf compels us to see the impact of the war on famously *logos*. Her concern of what language can do is featured through her practice with words.

Yet, the middle part of *To the Lighthouse* is less interested in exploring war on the battlefield or capturing the war experiences by using factual evidence than Proust is in *Le Temps retrouvé*. By including soldiers' letters and memories of the war, descriptions of the fighting, the Narrator receives from Gilberte and Saint-Loup, press articles and discussions held in the Parisian salons around the news coming from the fronts, Proust points at the ways in which the discourse of his contemporary civil society is corrupted. The way the language is employed in the political discourse appears to Proust as concealing the true motives of the war. He gives the example of those young and less aware people who get easily manipulated by patriotic expressions: "the Radical-Socialists who were, in a sense, unconscious patriots, independents, without a defined religion of patriotism, did not realise what a profound reality underlay what they believed to be vain and hateful formulas" (*Time Regained*: 41).[16] Proust challenges mechanized associations which, through the corrupted discourse, obstruct people from making informed decisions. He illustrates how the language of the mass-media can enhance aggression and hatred between people: "The truth is that people see everything through their newspaper and how can they do otherwise, seeing that they themselves know nothing about the peoples or the events in question" (*ibid.*: 71).[17] Proust even refers to the fake news problem: "Reading the papers, the triumphant tone of the articles daily representing Germany laid low, 'the beast at bay, reduced to impotence,' at a time when the contrary was only too true" (*Time Regained*: 65).[18] Reliable information is hard to find even in seemingly credible sources of information: "those who had announced years ago from a reliable source that negotiations for peace had begun, specifying even the clauses of the armistice, did not take the trouble, when they talked with you, to excuse themselves for their false information" (*Time Regained*: 66).[19]

Unlike Proust, Woolf does not provide the civilians' (and still less the combatant civilians') visions and experiences of the war in *TL*. However, she nestles the news coming from the fronts within brackets. Woolf marks her opposition to the propagandistic use of language with the bracketed text in the intermediary part of the novel. The deaths of the central character Mrs. Ramsay and her

---

[16] "les patriotes en quelque sorte inconscients, indépendants, sans religion patriotique définie, qu'étaient les radicaux-socialistes, n'avaient pas su comprendre quelle réalité profonde vivait dans ce qu'ils croyaient de vaines et haineuses formules," *Le Temps retrouvé*: 606-607.
[17] "La vérité c'est que les gens voient tout par leur journal, et comment pourraient-ils faire autrement puisqu'ils ne connaissent pas personnellement les gens ni les événements dont il s'agit?" *ibid.*: 640.
[18] "En lisant les journaux, l'air de triomphe des chroniqueurs présentent chaque jour l'Allemagne à bas, 'La Bête aux abois, réduite à l'impuissance,' alors que le contraire n'était que trop vrai [...]," *ibid.*: 633.
[19] "ceux qui avaient annoncé de source sûre, il y avait déjà plusieurs années, que les pourparlers de paix étaient commencés, spécifiant les clauses du traité, ne prenaient pas la peine quand ils causaient avec vous de s'excuser de leurs fausses nouvelles," *ibid.*: 634.

children Andrew and Prue are reported in brackets in "Time Passes" to articulate the painful sorrow in response to the stories of war as told in the newspapers. The bracketed deaths also suggest that words may fall short when describing life's cataclysmic incidents. Woolf uses the square brackets elsewhere in "Time Passes." The newspaper report is also placed in square brackets: "[Mr. Carmichael brought out a volume of poems that spring, which had an unexpected success. The war, people said, had revived their interest in poetry]" (*TL*: 153). By nestling this newspaper report within square brackets Woolf invites the reader to see that the news is loaded with propaganda which manipulates perspective (Levenback: 103). Certainly, there is no justification of war in the fact that people are reading poetry. However, we learn from the piece of information that the newspaper reporters seek to show that the war increases people's interest in poetry. There is an implied criticism of abuse of language in Woolf's own practice with words. She criticizes those academics who justify the aim of war while hoping "that the Fascist era would soon give birth to a poet worthy of it" (*AROO*: 86). The war has not given birth to new poets, but it helped the existing poet make an "unexpected success," as it is stated within brackets in *To the Lighthouse*.

In a similar vein as Proust, Woolf refers to photos, newspapers, manifestos, pamphlets and letters in *Three Guineas*, with the aim of expressing her deep concern with the growing violence in England and abroad. In her essay Woolf shows how the rhetorical power of visual language is exercised in support of the war. She refers to the photographs of dead bodies and ruined houses but deliberately avoids including them in her polemic: "those certainly are dead children, and that undoubtedly is the section of a house. A bomb has torn open the side" (*TG*: 14). By leaving the photographs out of *Three Guineas* Woolf implicitly invites us to pay attention to the rhetorical power that the photography yields. Ultimately, she offers the readers the rhetoric-free account of the war in Spain (Holly: 146).

If the essay *Three Guineas* clearly reacts against the corruption of language in the mouths of "fathers" and "brothers," the "Time Passes" section mirrors what the abuse of language entails. The middle section captures a decaying wreck of the world as time passes: "from the upper rooms of the empty house only gigantic chaos streaked with lightning could have been heard tumbling and tossing, as the winds and waves disported themselves like the amorphous bulks of leviathans whose brows are pierced by no light of reason, and mounted one on top of another and lunged and plunged in the darkness or the daylight" (*TL*: 154). It stages a true battle between cultural and primitive forms of life. We see that the upper-class Ramsays and their intellectual guests abandon the house to primitiveness, wilderness and darkness.

While Woolf expresses the war experiences with figurative language and bracketed text in *To the Lighthouse*, Proust is less reserved at dressing the images of violence. He compares the anarchy in the world to the violence within a family, salon or small society circles. One of the episodes in *Le Temps retrouvé* develops around the Narrator's discovery of a male brothel which at first appears to be a hotel. Marcel hears the talk of a man imploring someone's forgiveness: "there on the bed, like Prometheus bound to his rock, squirming under the strokes of a cat-o-nine-tails, which was, as a fact, loaded with nails, wielded by Maurice, already bleeding and covered with bruises which proved he was not submitting to the torture for the first time, I saw before me M. de Charlus" (*Time Regained*: 96).[20] This scene reveals to the Narrator that the Baron de Charlus is attracted to brutal men and enjoys a masochistic ordeal. The scene serves as evidence that not only does violence take place on a battle-field, but also behind closed shutters within such small groups of society as the male brothel is. Yet, if Charlus deliberately seeks out the torture, those fighting on the front do not. Marcel discovers not only Charlus, but Saint-Loup also attending the brothel and that the two are in love with the same man, Charlie Morel (artist, musician and soldier). It comes as a surprise to the Narrator to learn that Charlus, a distinguished man

---

[20] "[...] et là, enchaîné sur un lit comme Prométhée sur son rocher, recevant les coups d'un martinet en effet planté de clous que lui infligeait Maurice, je vis, déjà tout en sang, et couvert d'ecchymoses qui prouvaient que le supplice n'avait pas lieu pour la première fois, je vis devant moi M. de Charlus," *Le Temps retrouvé*: 678.

of the Faubourg St-Germain, spends time with men of lower classes just as Swann (with Odette) and the Narrator (with Albertine) do. He further learns that the brothel is attended by men from different social backgrounds, such as soldiers, the aristocracy and government members.

Proust labels the war as "the passionate romance of homosexuals" (*Time Regained*: 41),[21] affording unexpected opportunities to homosexuals despite the shortage of men. For a homosexual like Saint-Loup,

> [...] the war was [rather the very] ideal that he had imagined pursuing [...], to serve with beings he preferred, in a purely masculine chivalric order, far from women, where he could expose his life to save his orderly, and die inspiring fanatical love of his men" (*Time Regained*: 41)
>
> [...] la guerre fut davantage l'idéal même qu'il s'imaginait poursuivre [...], cet idéal servi en commun avec les êtres qu'il préférait, dans un ordre de chevalerie purement masculin, loin des femmes, où il pourrait exposer sa vie pour sauver son ordonnance, et mourir en inspirant un amour fanatique à ses hommes. (*Le Temps retrouvé*: 609)

Sodom embodies violence in *Le Temps retrouvé*. When the Narrator walks out of the brothel, he hears a bomb dropping nearby which reminds him of the eruption of Mount Vesuvius and the word "*Sodom and Gomorra*" (*Time Regained*, 89; *Le Temps retrouvé*, 657) written on the wall in Pompei by the inhabitants, representative of an apocalyptic vision. Sodom, forbidden passions, hold central place in the fourth volume of *Sodome et Gomorrhe (Sodom and Gomorrah)*, as well. Yet, to the last volume *Time Regained* Proust adds accounts of homosexual love promoted by the war.

Proust and Woolf appear as opponents of the propagandistic use of language also because they refuse to generalize the effects of the war catastrophes. Woolf reduces the scale of the Great War to the size of the Ramsays' family house. Proust also explains the nature of the war by studying it within the small circles of society. He found the nature of conflict between people and nations was similar and explained that "a fight [is] born only of a conflict

---

[21] "le roman passionné des homosexuels," *ibid.*, p. 609.

between two characters" (*Time Regained*: 61).²² According to Proust: "The logic which governs them is within them and is perpetually remoulded by passion like that of people engaged in a love-quarrel or in some domestic dispute, such as that of a son with his father, of a cook with her mistress, of a woman with her husband" (*ibid.*: 63).²³ Thus, Proust shows that the reason for war is rooted in domestic violence.

We saw that Proust and Woolf also avoided describing the First World War in its immediacy. Yet, they try to find a language in tune with its destructive scale. Through the use of figurative language and brackets in *To the Lighthouse*, Woolf shows that death in the context of war is unspeakable. Proust is more direct in his criticism of the propagandistic use of language. He dresses the images of violence within Jupien's male brothel. Whipping Charlus with "ferocious accessories obtained with greatest difficulty even from sailors (the punishment they used to inflict having been abolished even where the discipline is strictest, on ship-board),"²⁴ *ibid.*: 115) mirrors the violence on the battlefield, in a wider sense: "At such moments of insanity [M. de Charlus] knew perfectly well that the man who was beating him was no wickeder than the little boys in battle-games who draw lots to decide which of them is to play the Prussian and upon whom all the others fall in true patriotic ardour and pretended hatred" (*ibid.*: p. 114).²⁵ We also learned that

---

[22] "[...] il existe d'énormes entassements organisés d'individus qu'on appelle nations; leur vie ne fait que répéter en les amplifiant la vie des cellules composantes [...] ces masses colossales d'individus conglomérés s'affrontant l'une l'autre prendront [...] une beauté plus puissante que la lutte naissant seulement du conflit de deux caractères [...]," *Le Temps retrouvé*: 629.

[23] "La logique qui les conduit est tout intérieure, et perpétuellement refondue par la passion, comme celle de gens affrontés dans une querelle amoureuse ou domestique, comme la querelle d'un fils avec son père, d'une cuisinière avec sa patronne, d'une femme avec son mari," *ibid.*: 631.

[24] "[...] des accessoires féroces qu'on avait la plus grande peine à se procurer même en s'adressant à des matelots–car ils servaient à infliger des supplices dont l'usage est aboli même là où la discipline est la plus rigoureuse, à bord des navires [...]," *ibid.*: 682.

[25] "Ce fou savait bien, malgré tout, qu'il était la proie d'une folie et jouait tout de même, dans ces moments-là, puisqu'il savait bien que celui qui le battait n'était pas plus méchant que le petit garçon qui dans les jeux de bataille est désigné au

Proust and Woolf merge the artistic with the political. They avoid grasping the reality of the war on the battlefield. Instead, they adopt aesthetic strategies compatible with the horror of their contemporary history and challenge the mechanized associations corrupting the public discourse.

References

Primary sources

Proust, Marcel. *À la Recherche du temps perdu*. 3 : *La prisonnière, La fugitive (Albertine disparue), Le temps retrouvé*. Paris: Robert Laffont, 1987.

Proust, Marcel. *Time Regained*, tr. Stephen Hudson. London: Chatto & Windus, 1931. Available online: http://gutenberg.net.au

Woolf, Virginia. *A Room of One's Own* (1929). San Diego: Harcourt Brace, 1989. (Cited as *AROO*).

Woolf, Virginia. "Crafstmanship," in *Selected Essays*, ed. Bradshaw, David. Oxford: Oxford University Press, 2008. (Cited as *SE*)

Woolf, Virginia. "On Not Knowing Greek" (1925), in *Virginia Woolf: A Woman's Essays*, ed. Bowlby, Rachel. Harmondsworth: Penguin, 1992: 93-106.

Woolf, Virginia. *The Common Reader* (Second Series). London: The Hogarth Press, 1953. (Cited as *CR*).

Woolf, Virginia. *The Letters of Virginia Woolf*, vol. II, 1912-1922, ed. Nicolson, Nigel. New York: Houghton Brace Jovanovich, 1976: 525.

Woolf, Virginia. "The Novels of E. M. Forster" (1927), in *The Death of the Moth and Other Essays*. London: Hogarth Press, 1942: 106-107.

Woolf, Virginia. *Three Guineas* (1938), annotated and introduced by Marcus, Jane. Orlando: Harcourt, 2006. (Cited as *TG*.)

Woolf, Virginia. "To Margaret Llewelyn Davies" (February 9, 1925), in *The Letters of Virginia Woolf*, vol. III: 1923-28, ed. Nicolson, Nigel and Trautmann, Joanne. London: Hogarth Press, 1977: 166.

Woolf, Virginia (1927). *To the Lighthouse*. Introduction by Julia Briggs. New York: A. A. Knopf, 1992. (Cited as *TL*.)

Woolf, Virginia. *To the Lighthouse: The Original Holograph Draft*. Transcribed and edited by Dick, Susan. Toronto: University of Toronto Press, 1982. (Cited as *OHD*).

---

sort pour faire le 'Prussien', et sur lequel tout le monde se rue dans une ardeur de patriotisme vrai et de haine feinte," *ibid.*: 681.

Secondary sources

Barbakadze, Tamar. "Catherine Colomb et Virginia Woolf. 'Raconter' la guerre à travers des métaphores," in *Esthétique de la guerre - Éthique de la paix. Un siècle de littérature sur la Grande Guerre*, eds. Jochen Mecke, Pierre Schoentjes, Anne-Sophie Donnarieix. Paris: Classiques Garnier, 2021: 163-176.

Haule, M. James. "'Le Temps passe' and the Original Typescript: an Early Version of the 'Time Passes' Section of *To the Lighthouse*," in *Twentieth-Century Literature*, Vol. 29, No. 3, Duke University Press (Autumn, 1983): 267-311.

Hoare, Dorothy M. *Some Studies in the Modern Novel*. London: Chatto and Windus, 1938.

Holly, Henry. *Virginia Woolf and the Discourse of Science*. Cambridge: Cambridge University Press, 2003.

Levenback, Karen L., *Virginia Woolf and the Great War*. New York: Syracuse University Press, 1999.

Philippe, Gilles. *French Style. L'accent français de la prose anglaise*. Bruxelles: Les impressions nouvelles, 2016.

Tratner, Michael. *Modernism and Mass Politics: Joyce, Woolf, Eliot, Yeats*. Stanford: Stanford University Press, 1995.

Zwerding, Alex. *Virginia Woolf and the Real World*. Berkeley: California University Press, 1986.

The Discreet Charm of Refraining from Judgment.
A Few Doubts Concerning Evaluation in Contemporary Literary Criticism

Olga Szmidt (Jagiellonian University)

There is a series of scenes in the film *The Discreet Charm of the Bourgeoisie* in which a group of middle-aged couples faces various obstacles preventing them from enjoying dinner and satisfying declared hunger. Among ten obstacles, as specified by Juan Roberto Mora Catlett, there are death, police raids, "a battalion of soldiers," forgetfulness and realizing that one is on the theatre's stage instead of in the dining room (Mora Catlett, 1999: 56). The artificiality of the world created by Buñuel is not merely a convention. It breaks through into the material world—rubber poultry matches hunger suppression with class ritual. "They are condemned to it for eternity," notes Mora Catlett (1999: 57). Eating itself becomes a negligible aspect of dinner as its linguistic presence in a conversation replaces food. Unlike in the film directed by Buñuel two years later, *The Phantom of Liberty*, eating is not yet a secret concealed with shame. It is rather the excluded centre of the ritual. The unfulfilled promise of dinner creates tension, but it is more a frustration of incomplete ritual rather than being hungry. The characters are looking for ideal conditions, a perfect context that would exclude their own guilt (about distributing drugs, marital infidelity, etc.), and at the same time cleanse the reality of any sort of dissonance (mortality, violence, politics, morality). The dinner thus becomes an unattainable reward.

The hopelessness of carrying it out could gradually damage the status of the characters but paradoxically strengthens it. In the penultimate scene, we see the survivor of the shooting feasting under the table. He is ultimately betrayed by his hunger. Released from the gaze of others, he is not only unable to hold back anymore, but also risks his life to fulfil the excluded centre of the ritual. *The Discreet Charm of the Bourgeoisie* can be annoying and frustrating for the viewer — like an endless delay of the dinner. In all this surreal impossibilism, what seems striking is not the observation that middle-class rituals overshadow fundamental human needs and class struggle. Quite the contrary; the status-sustaining ritual is not threatened, precisely because its fulfilment is unattainable. Empty ritual is the fullest and most spectacular form of ritual. It is not its downfall, but the realization of its single purpose: to maintain order.

One might wonder what the film directed by Luis Buñuel 50 years ago has to do with literary criticism. Besides the parabolic potential of the film, it can be used as an excellent way to shed more light on challenges and inherited problems that literary criticism faces today. While the spirit of literary criticism is both subversive and, to quote Terry Eagleton, "born of a struggle against the absolute state" (Eagleton, 2005: 9), it is at the same time burdened with many rituals that often effectively conceal its potential. The decades-old hesitation on what grounds and what protocols the critic should offer any kind of judgment or evaluation, resulted (among other things) in diverse definitions of literary criticism in various languages and cultural and academic contexts. W. W. Robson observes in the 80s that

> Literary criticism has traditionally been regarded as evaluative, or judicial. But over the centuries this notion of it has come to be questioned, and itself "evaluated" adversely. [...] Is the idea of evaluative criticism really compatible with rational discussion, as that is understood nowadays? Does it belong with other, now discredited ideas of authority in regions of discourse where no authority can respectably exist? (Robson, 1982: 40)

Although Robson defends a rather traditional model of literature and seems to be dissatisfied with the development of the discipline, he rightly states that withdrawing from evaluative criticism resulted in diverse approaches to analysing literature (Robson, 1982: 43-47). It can therefore be said that withdrawal from evaluation was a liberating stage for literary criticism. This function, however, turned out to be much more permanently embedded in its socio-cultural status than one might expect. In many cultures it did not disappear in the same way or as quickly. This variety of characterizations should not be overlooked, either theoretically, or culturally. Depending on the conceptual framework in which we operate, we encounter both various principles of the field and an understanding of who the people that describe themselves or are referred to as literary critics are. What is more, the default audiences of their articles would be put in question, as well as limits of their criticism (Felski, 2015: 8-10). We would probably also recognize a range of roles which the critics are about to play in forming and transforming the literary canon. These variances will therefore influence the means that we assign to literary criticism especially in the face of the challenge that World Literature presents today.

Ambiguity and asynchrony of literary criticism

The theory of criticism, as René Wellek observed in the 60s, had not been a field that could be described as extensive or historically influential (Wellek, 1963: 21). Quite the contrary. While the term "criticism" is widely used in different contexts, academic and beyond, literary criticism does not attract a notable crowd of theorists. Since the publication of Wellek's famous book, certain developments in the meta-criticism or theory of literary criticism field are noticeable. Even if we remain in the English-language context, we should mention the works of Stanley Fish, Norman N. Holland, Terry Eagleton, Peter Uwe Hohendahl, Harold Bloom and critics inspired by Northrop Frye's scholarship, and, in a slightly different domain, Catherine Belsey. In a broader perspective, German researchers should be included as well. We should mention, among others, Wolfgang Iser and Hans Robert Jauss, as well as many interpreters of Walter Benjamin's work. Nonetheless, creating such a list seems to have limited functionality, given the connectivity of literary criticism with other disciplines and research trends in an interdisciplinary or transdisciplinary approach, as well as literary criticism's habit of borrowing tools from other spheres of literary research. In the above context, one should ask whether

Wellek's great work, *A History of Modern Criticism 1750-1950*[1] (Wellek, 1955-1992), will be carried on by others to this day and whether it would be possible to rework it for the "World Literary Criticism" version.

Apart from these highly influential works, one could easily find numerous articles and monographs devoted to particular dilemmas (ethical, theoretical, sociological, etc.) and interdisciplinary areas such as translation criticism. A few examples, outstanding as they might be, cannot, however, obscure the fact that the practice and theory of criticism have constantly appeared in the puzzling context of definitional ambiguity. The history of the term compiled by Wellek, dating back to antiquity and revised many times afterward, shows the process of judgment or evaluation as the basis for distinguishing this field (Wellek, 1963: 22-25). The fact that we are still discussing the issue of evaluation in literary criticism shows, on the one hand, the persistence of this concept, and on the other, its significant variability. One could say that criticism is defined not only by differentiating it from related domains (rhetoric, grammar, poetics), but also by how it gradually becomes a domain in itself[2].

One could mention the similarity of the German and Polish understanding of criticism[3]. However, in the latter case the

---

[1] One could find it interesting that a similar monograph on the Polish history of literary criticism was edited by Jan Zygmunt Jakubowski almost simultaneously. While Wellek chose 1950 as a final date for his project, Jakubowski's edition contains two volumes: respectively 1800-1918 and 1919-1939 (Jakubowski 1959, 1966).

[2] Wellek notices that for English criticism a very important step was the addition of the suffix '-ism' (Wellek 1963: 27-28)–something that has no analogy, for example, in the Polish language. "Krytyka" (criticism) is both a word describing a humanistic field and an act of expressing a judgment, not necessarily in the literary context.

[3] In the Polish case, it had not caused analogous devaluation due to significantly different historical contexts such as Polish intellectuals' engagement in public affairs. Besides, German literary culture's development is described by Wellek in a negatively charged way, which is not necessary the case on the other side of the Oder River. The author underlines the decline of literary criticism in the German institutional context: "A divorce between aesthetics, a philosophical discipline to which poetics was subordinated, and literary scholarship, which was mainly literary history, became a feature of the German intellectual scene

borderline between literary criticism and literary research grows larger and larger in the following decades; contemporarily it reaches its height. As Janusz Sławiński observed yet in the 70s:

> Hardly anyone today harbours illusions as to the possibility of drawing a clear line between the domain of truly critical statements and the domain of statements representing pure literary studies; in fact, they constantly interpenetrate, even when it comes to criticism that definitely manifests its aversion to "science," and on the other hand, literary studies that have this "science" written on their banner. (Sławiński, 1974: 11)

While the structuralist dispute over the "scientific" pretentions of the humanities seems to be somewhat out of date today, it seems to return to the critics' judgment of literature. The uncertain status of a usurper discipline is therefore in question. These doubts also reappear as an argument against this borderline, interdisciplinary and essentially ambiguous discipline and its domain. Around the same time another critic sharing an idealistic approach to the discipline wrote that

> Above all, a critic represents literature's cause. He[4] acts on behalf of all the literary works which have already been created and can be created. To put it more broadly, he acts on behalf of culture as a whole. That is why he is both ignorant and over-learned. He combines and mixes everything with everything: personal confessions with game theory, ethnology with poetics, and psychology with semiology... but in an extremely capricious, accidental and messy way. [...] The scientist[5] accuses the critic of arbitrariness, the critic accuses the scientist of dogmatism. (Błoński, 1978: 10)

The linguistic ambiguity among the contradictory ideas of literary criticism in the international perspective becomes noteworthy if we examine their meaning in several European languages such as Polish *krytyka literacka*, German *Literaturkritik*

---

of the nineteenth century. The critic became a mere middleman, a journalist of ephemeral significance." (Wellek 1963: 32)

[4] I am translating here directly from Polish, in which gender forms are much more present than in English. Nowadays, the term "critic, that is, him" is also often used in the supposedly universal meaning. In recent years, there has been a significant change here — in favor of the double gender forms, less often the plural form. In the context of Błoński's article, however, it can be concluded that the author uses the traditional form of a critic as a man, but not exclusively a man.

[5] As a scientist Błoński understands here academics from the field of literary studies, especially structuralists, i.e. the aforementioned Janusz Sławiński.

and Russian литературная критика. Primarily, they denote various reviewing practices aimed at a wide range of readers. There are also more ambiguous cases, such as French understanding of *la critique littéraire*,[6] related to the condition of the entire literary studies and their socio-cultural context. It is worth noting, however, that even in the Polish context a significant expansion of declaratively non-evaluative criticism can be observed in recent years (Bolecki, Burek, Jarzębski, Markowski, Stala, Wyka, 2007: 411-422). This development can be attributed to the growing influence of English-language literary criticism worldwide, but also to the need to strengthen critical meta-reflection. Another factor here, as in many universities, is the emphasis on literary theory and theoretical inspirations for interpretation practices (Cieślak-Sokołowski, 2007: 377-379). Nevertheless, I would be more inclined to attach greater importance to the first of these reasons, namely globalization of both literary culture and the academic world.

While working on another article, I accidentally came across an essay (written in Polish) in which an author rivetingly declares that she connects the definition of translation criticism with the term "literary criticism" as understood in English while using both of the terms in her native Polish language (Kraskowska, 2018: 54). Homi Bhabha would probably call it an "unhomely moment" (Bhabha, 1992: 141). Hence, Kraskowska uses translation criticism's tools to adopt the foreign meaning without directly adopting the foreign words. Many researchers might find this a trivial dispute. Nonetheless, I believe that it concerns a symptomatic problem of cultural and theoretical asynchrony, occasionally evened out in a gesture of self-reflective translation. It seems, therefore, that the problem of ambiguity lies not necessarily (or not only) in the translation dissimilarities and historical development of literary

---

[6] René Wellek elaborates on that issue: "In France, in spite of the prestige of Sainte-Beuve and Taine, the meaning of the word 'critique' has narrowed somewhat, though later than in Germany, for different reasons, and with less drastic effects. [...] The hostility to criticism is rather a peculiarity of the French academic situation and the positivistic factualism so conspicuous in its doctrine of comparative literature than a widely shared contraction of the term 'critique'" (34-35).

studies, but also in the assessment of the status and condition of literary criticism. As an auxiliary in defining translation criticism, Katharina Reiss offers her observations on the related field of literary criticism, particularly German literary criticism. She seems to follow the path of negative evaluation of literary criticism, traditionally understood in Germany as reviewing practices:[7]

> It has been remarked often enough that with the advent of commercialization in the literary world, the level of literary criticism (apart from some outstanding exceptions) has generally sunk alarmingly low. (Reiss, 2014: 1)

Hence, portraying literary criticism in an unflattering light encourages the author to put translation criticism side by side with the "adopted meaning" of English literary criticism, quite like the above-mentioned Polish author. Particularly in this context it seems puzzling that the German theorist in her approach to translation criticism focuses so intensely on the process of evaluation and value-judgment which are traditionally attributed to the discipline from which she distances herself. Interestingly, however, she develops a near-scientific evaluation protocol that aims for the highest possible objectivity (Reiss, 2014: 1-8) with the translation critic aspiring to be a translator's guide and teacher (Reiss, 2014: 15). It is meant to be a counter-answer to the nonchalant practices of literary critics based mostly on their whims and idiosyncrasies (Reiss, 2014: 9).

Evaluation and judgment as detached features of literary criticism

In addition to the above-discussed dilemmas, the historical variability of the concept of literary criticism does not enable a simple recognition that the semantic field delineated by the English

---

[7] Wellek sees dangers in literary reviewing in a broader sense: "The German narrowing to daily book reviewing seems to me dangerous because it leaves evaluation to the journalist and isolates 'Literaturwissenschaft' as a discipline removed from contemporary literature and released from the task of discrimination and evaluation." (Wellek, 1963: 35-36)

understanding is either universally applicable or ultimate. It seems, however, that in the context of, for example, American and British literary criticism, a certain variety of definitions and goals can be observed too. Consequently, there is also a significant diversity of attitudes towards withdrawing from evaluation as a function of literary criticism. An example of this discussion can be found in an article by Alexander Larman in "The Critic." The essay is stylized practically as a manifesto, as it proclaims a flat-out disappointment in literary criticism in view of its lack of clear assessments and judgments about reviewed literature. The author discusses this topic from the writer's perspective, but he seems to be preoccupied with this dilemma as a committed press reader:

> I had to read [John] Carey's review twice to find out what his opinion of what he had reviewed was, meanwhile. He describes it as "illuminating" in the first paragraph, and then in the last paragraph offers the detail that "[Toby] Musgrave's claim that Banks changed our world is not an exaggeration." Other than that, the thousand-word-long article was devoted to a précis of what was in the book, summarising Banks' achievements in brief form. [...] I would have hoped that any critic, whether one as knowledgeable as [Denis] Donoghue or someone further down the food chain, would be able to deal with the merits and virtues, or the flaws, of the book in an interesting and original fashion. (Larman, 2020)

Larman goes on to suggest that critics' withdrawal from judgment is at least partly caused by the devaluation of literary culture in the press. It provides them with lower wages and less space in the daily and specialist press. It would be really difficult to disagree with this diagnosis, which only proves that the institution of criticism is not only in a figurative but also in a quite real economic crisis. Alongside, it seems that Larman rightly notices that reading literary reviews which do not offer evaluation directly or in a more subtle way, seems to be quite a peculiar activity. It is worth emphasizing that he does not call for simple measures or reducing criticism to unsophisticated grading. Rather, he urges critics not to shy away from this role. Interestingly, Larman points out how much linguistic rituals, euphemisms and futile summaries overshadow a lack of conclusion. These formulaic statements do not typically suggest that a critic hesitates as to how to evaluate a given novel (which from my personal perspective is extremely rare, and could be beneficially disclosed more often) but ritually camouflages it. In other words: in this perspective the critic conceals his or her judgment and creates an aura of mystery around not judging the book directly. It would be a mistake, however, to consider this diagnosis as unique to our era.

If Larman's article uses the form of a manifesto or an appeal in some passages, then Elizabeth Hardwick's essay from sixty years ago should be called a passionate pamphlet. The piece, originally published in *Harper's Magazine*, is today a classic that spurred the founding of one of the journals defining contemporary criticism — the *New York Review of Books* (Danner, Silvers, 2013). Although she comments mostly on a then-dominant force in American literary criticism — the *New York Times'* literary section — Hardwick states:

> Sweet, bland commendations fall everywhere upon the scene; a universal, if somewhat lobotomized, accommodation reigns. A book is born into a puddle of treacle; the brine of hostile criticism is only a memory. Everyone is found to have "filled a need," and is to be "thanked" for something and to be excused for "minor faults in an otherwise excellent work." [...] The worst result of its decline is that it acts as a sort of hidden dissuader, gently, blandly, respectfully denying whatever vivacious interest there might be in books or literary matters generally. The flat praise and the faint dissension, the minimal style and the light little article, the absence of involvement, passion, character, eccentricity — the lack, at last, of the literary tone itself — have made the *New York Times* into a provincial literary journal [...]. (Hardwick, 1959)

Hardwick not only recognizes the worthlessness of bland praise, recognition devoid of enthusiasm, and general averaging of ratings (Felski, 2015: 8) but also points to the fact that criticism is entwined in the publishing market. What appears to be specific to our day, and as such is noted with horror by many commentators,[8] seems from this perspective as a recurrent tug of war:

> [...] the book world is being slowly, painlessly killed. Everything is somehow alike, whether it be a routine work of history by a respectable

---

[8] It is worth noting in this context that one of the discussions that invigorated Polish literary critics in recent years was devoted to the issue of evaluation and the disappearance of literary disputes (Jakubowiak, 2016; Cieślik, 2016; Orliński, 2016).

> academic, a group of platitudes from the Pentagon, a volume of verse, a work of radical ideas, a work of conservative ideas. Simple "coverage" seems to have won out over the drama of opinion; "readability," a cosy little word, has taken the place of the old-fashioned requirement of a good, clear prose style, which is something else. All differences of excellence, of position, of form are blurred by the slumberous acceptance. (Hardwick, 1959)

Even though Larman reflected on avoiding judgments in favour of indifferent reviewers' appreciation for "interesting" or "illuminating" novels (I would add a different keyword here: "novels engaging in socially important topics"), this diagnosis seems to be a consistent next step in relation to Hardwick's diagnosis half a century earlier. To come back to the parallel with Buñuel's film—evaluation cannot emerge in the text, nor can food during the dinner. They are merely pretexts for communication and for creating a socio-cultural ritual. The review does not have to fulfil its basic role, not necessarily in a gesture of critical refinement, but in a gesture of safeguarding literary criticism's fading authority. Since the evaluation has little or no function or is merely a mock-up, it must eventually fade away. Consequently, the process of fully withdrawing from judgment seems to be a natural consequence. As literary history has shown (for instance in the aforementioned form of a newly established journal) this is not an irreversible process and should not be approached fatalistically. It seems that the moment of recognizing the crisis is crucial for this process. Not necessarily as a moment of wringing hands over a lost Golden Age (which, as one can see, not only never really took place, but which in each epoch becomes an operational figure for recognizing today's crisis). In that case we could say that the nostalgic observations expressed during yet another crisis of literary criticism reveal aspects of this field which need to be updated. In other words: what is truly lost and why it is not necessarily a bad thing. In the context of the crisis we face a unique chance not only to re-evaluate the principles, but also identify what rituals of ours only served to maintain the worn-out ritual. Looking from this perspective, we could realize that shielding is not actually the best strategy for surviving this crisis. Contrariwise, we might benefit from taking a risk.

One could argue that this kind of observations and perspectives on critics' role at least partly supports the process of "professorisation" of literary criticism—namely, the domination of academic literary researchers over literary criticism. As Peter Uwe Hohendahl observes:

> This division between the academy and the press is not unknown in the United States and has at least to some extent shaped the mode of American literary criticism. Yet this impact has been less forceful, since the literary critic as a journalist is a model that has been less successful here than in Europe. The academic critic has assumed many of the functions that are exercised by the free-lance critic, the publicist, in France or Germany. Reviewers for the *New York Review of Books* are usually university professors at more or less distinguished institutions. (Hohendahl, 2016: 14)

Another reason in favour of reconsidering the theory of literary criticism in the latter half of the 20th century is the need to revise the foundations on which we are building contemporary and future literary criticism—in terms of its principles, its funding worldviews in different cultures, and, last but not least, detailed issues such as the necessity or redundancy of evaluation as a function of this discourse. To outline contemporary questions, it is worth considering to what extent traditional literary criticism responds to contemporary literary challenges. It seems worth asking whether the independence of literary criticism from academia, characteristic of German or Polish culture (Hohendahl, 2016: 14-18), is necessarily its curse and weakness (Wellek, 1963: 35). In this context, one might have some doubts around the category of "common sense," both implicitly and explicitly used by literary critics of different occupations. This category not only supports expressive realism over other conventions and poetics, but also forces the interpreter to use various types of "obviousness" (Belsey, 1980: 2-5). An extensive usage of this category undoubtedly threatens the freedom and originality of interpretation, and therefore affects the condition of contemporary criticism which is seen as redundant, strictly dependent on other literary studies and literature itself (Sławiński, 1979: 6-7). Contrarily, Catherine Belsey suggests recognizing a certain agenda of a literary work (namely its worldview, otherwise referred to as ideology) in order to then free the text from the expectations of the reader of realistic literature. She states that

> Such a criticism does not simply reject the classic realist text as an object of consumption, imposing a form of censorship on the mode of writing which remains dominant in our society, but works to foreground its contradiction and so to read it radically. Such a criticism finds in the literary work a new object of intelligibility: it produces the text. (Belsey, 1980: 129)

Belsey does not separate critical practice from literary theory; instead, she tries to combine the "non-obviousness" of a literary text with the "non-obviousness" of criticism. She therefore rejects the idea that what seems familiar has to be the truth (Belsey, 1980: 3). Thus expressed scepticism towards the primacy of expressive realism as a worldview based on trusting to "familiar assumptions" (Belsey, 1980: 5) is a promising prospect. She argues that expressive realism based on common sense is a kind of tautology — it reflects the experience of the world that has already been developed linguistically and is, in fact, previously known to us (Belsey, 1980: 46). In such case, the role of criticism is to challenge the obvious and the socio-literary consensus that enabled this literary work. Alternatively, in the case of works that seem to radically break the narrative and linguistic patterns known to us so far, we can often observe various strategies of critical helplessness, polite recognition of the idiomatic text, or even omitting the title in a critical selection of the issues discussed. The primacy of common sense is directly related to a clear preference for texts written not only in a realistic convention, but those which encourage autobiographical approach. It enables replacing the interpretation with a conversation about the author, their experience, the cultural and political contexts of the novel. A resourceful critic is able to do it almost seamlessly, but this does not change the fact that such work should be regarded to a large extent as derivative, often redundant. Few critics are willing to use heavy interpretive weapons, fearing perhaps not so much a dispute with other reviewers, but to reveal their own discomfiture towards a work that turned out to be simply mismatched with the interpretative tools at their disposal. I would venture to say that this is often the cause of polite recommendations and barely argued dissatisfaction. Not an affirmation of our differences and diversity, but of indifference and critical withdrawal.

Dysfunction of literary criticism and the prospect of refraining from judgment

In this article, I discuss mostly the theories and discussions either from the second part of the 20th century or rooted in this decades' ideas. The reasons for such a choice, however, are relatively obvious. According to René Wellek, both theory and history of literary criticism have been far from a crowded field (Wellek 1963: 21). Especially in recent decades, one can observe a shift in the devotion of literary theorists and critics to other fields and issues In this context, it seems necessary to note that the very term literary criticism, even if we take into account only the contemporary context, is marked by ambiguity. It seems obvious that New Criticism will be radically different from Marxist criticism, feminist from structuralist, post-deconstructive from the Geneva School. So how can we use the general concept of literary criticism at all and what is the point of this, one could say, theoretical fiction? The answer to this question, however, is pleasantly simple: their common place is institution of criticism. Peter Uwe Hohendahl shortly defines it as "the social models which guide and control the activity called literary criticism" (Hohendahl, 2016: 12). He recognizes "the university and the press" (Hohendahl, 2016: 14) as two disjoint institutional contexts shaping this discourse. Furthermore, Terry Eagleton critically examines the mentioned institution and its groundless stability:

> A critic may write with assurance as long as the critical institution itself is thought to be unproblematical. Once that institution is thrown into radical question, then one would expect individual acts of criticism to become troubled and self-doubting. The fact that such acts continue today, apparently in all their traditional confidence, is doubtless a sign that the crisis of the critical institution has either not been deeply enough registered, or is being actively evaded. (Eagleton, 2005: 7)

Although Terry Eagleton, while facing the meta-critical dilemma himself, argues "that criticism today lacks all substantive social function" (Eagleton, 2005: 7), he declares there is hope of recuperating its social importance. Even though Eagleton's book was written almost forty years ago, which is also revealed in the extensive polemics with New Criticism, is still crucial for the theory of literary criticism. I have the impression that he faultlessly, even if selectively, diagnosed systemic causes of the crisis of the discipline:

> I began this essay by arguing that modern criticism was born of a struggle against the absolutist state. It has ended up, in effect, as a handful of individuals reviewing each other's books. Criticism itself has become incorporated into the culture industry, as a "type of unpaid public relations, part of requirements in any large corporate undertaking" (Hohendahl 1976: 7). In the early eighteenth century, to risk an excessive generalization, criticism concerned cultural politics; in the nineteenth century its preoccupation was public morality; in our own century, it is a matter of "literature." [...] Yet it is arguable that criticism was only ever significant when it engaged with more than literary issues — when, for whatever historical reason, the "literary" was suddenly foregrounded as the medium of vital concerns deeply rooted in the general intellectual, cultural and political life of an epoch. (Eagleton, 2005: 107)

It can be argued that the idea of criticism that Eagleton endorses is gaining momentum today. Since contemporary literary criticism is directly involved in issues that ignite public discourse — issues of social inequality, representation of minorities and the problem of representation in general, gender and queer issues, or even the climate crisis — we could acknowledge that Eagleton's hopes of a renewal of criticism and its institution have been fulfilled. I must confess that, however tempting this optimistic conclusion would be, I am not sure if this is actually true.

In this respect, it should be noted that in the 21st century the crisis of literary criticism does not seem to be an overlooked topic. I would even risk a statement that the crisis has become a natural state of contemporary criticism. The recurring meta-reflection on weakness, crisis, and the fall of criticism may seem very radical, even revolutionary. This is not the case, however, as it has quickly become a ritual of passivity and powerlessness. In this context, Rita

Felski argues that we need to "expand our repertoire of critical moods while embracing a richer array of critical methods" (Felski, 2015: 13). The rules of criticism—and thus its institution itself—often seem to be an exciting, morally burdened call for waking up from the lethargy into which we have fallen into at least two decades ago. Surprisingly this cry concerns the demand to conduct heated discussions, to restore fervent judgments, the need to once again "quarrel over literature" (Jakubowiak, 2016). Implicitly—as was the case in the Golden Age. I understand this argument primarily as a longing for establishing the principle for the 20th-century literary criticism stated by Eagleton ("in our own century it is a matter of 'literature,'" Eagleton, 2005: 107). It does not seem surprising, therefore, that such a raked-up ideal of criticism does not live any longer and does not spark a revolution. This kind of statement temporarily consolidates nostalgic critics who long to rush for each other's throats and for a short period embarrasses reviewers who do not have a polemical temperament. Even so, we should not easily classify it as an unequivocally trivial dispute.

To follow Eagleton's venturesome epochal generalization, I'd say that as of now literary criticism seems to deal primarily with the issue of valuation. Not necessarily with the process of critical evaluation itself, but mainly with the dilemmas that arise around valuation. Therefore, one could say that this is a symptom of a larger problem–meta-reflection on criticism is a key dilemma of our new era. The fundamental question that we recurrently ask ourselves is whether we should judge at all.

This issue applies not only to the literary field but also to the progressive concealment of the language of evaluation in favour of the language of acceptance and accessibility. Seeing the potential benefits that this cultural shift can bring, we should carefully examine this problem. It is extremely demanding to argue with hidden judgments, and therefore very difficult to change, negotiate, and nuance them in the process of discussion. Risking a generalization I would say that for many critics an essay or even a review often creates a space perfectly described by Helen Vendler while answering a question concerning her audience: "No, I write to explain things to myself" (Vendler, 1996). It is worth pointing out that this phrase does not mean the same thing as explaining to others, let alone understanding or assimilating. Explaining to oneself not only means that the text requires interpretation (because it is not obvious), but that the reader can discover the process and, as Daniel Mendelsohn discloses, be drawn into a more complex relationship with literature (Mendelsohn, 2012). In this perspective, the central problem lays not necessarily in withdrawing from evaluation in a gesture of blunt affirmation—but in relegating evaluation to the domain of solipsistic and, above all, private experience. If this was to be the cause of the death of literary criticism, it would be a silent and, unlike the spirit of the discipline itself, a non-public event.

An additional aspect of judgment-withdrawal in literary criticism is the growing importance and diversity of World Literature. The expectation of a limited volume of text, as for a review or a catalogue rather than a proper piece of literary criticism, urges the critic to offer some general information, to bring out its most important topics, perhaps similarities to other publications. In other words: to introduce a title to an audience rather than offer an edgy interpretation. Therefore, paradoxically, the awareness of the complexity of World Literature puts the critic in a tricky position. Nonetheless, one could say that literary criticism towards World Literature (especially in translation) requires not only slightly different literary and linguistic competencies than discussing culturally closer authors, but the evaluation itself is justifiably the subject of reserved and careful reflection.

One could get the impression that the influence of World Literature not only finds resonance in discussions of foreign prose but has influenced the entire field of literary criticism. Caution in passing judgment seems to be a value that will not be easy to render if we focus on the history of this discipline. Among the insightful volumes and impressive essays we find more troubling, non-episodic cases. By that I do not mean only well-known mistakes and blind assessments, but also the malicious annihilation and butchering of literary works, as well as regretful prejudices about non-Western cultures, especially postcolonial ones (Gołuch, 2016), or non-male and non-heteronormative identities (Kowalcze-Pawlik, 2010).

The ethical aspect of refraining from evaluation is worth emphasizing in this context. It seems that there are at least two fundamental risks here. I consider the first to be the possibility of critics putting themselves in a condescending position towards literature they are not familiar with.[9] The strategy of refraining from judgment does not usually take the form of actual abstention from evaluation, nor lack of enjoyment (Fisher, 1968: 135-139), but rather results in an elaborate ritual of delineating the boundary between cultures, languages, and identities. There is also a different strategy associated with this boundary-setting ritual: positioning oneself as culturally transparent as opposed to the unfamiliar, the unknown, the Other which cannot be understood. From the perspective of the World Literature project, this seems particularly disturbing (McInturff, 2003: 224-236; Apter, 2013).

As the second risk of such a withdrawn strategy, I would label the deadlock in the transformation of the canon. It seems that in

---

[9] If written from the Western perspective it is often simply "non-Western" literature, often understood even as non-English literature. To use Zhang Longxi's phrase, World Literature has been operating in the optics of "the West and the Rest" (Longxi, 2018: 179). This term is quite accurate as it highlights hegemony rather than hierarchy. In this context, it seems that English domination as a global literature language is quite ambiguous. Longxi observes: "For our world today, there is no question that English is the most widely used language, a contemporary lingua franca used probably by more non-native than native speakers in the world today. As a consequence, then, works written in English have a better chance of circulating globally in the original, and works written in other languages could become known and circulate beyond their culture of origin if they are translated into English. Some scholars resent this "hegemony" of English, and some comparatists, with their disciplinary emphasis on working with the original, object to world literature that makes translation a necessary component" (Longxi, 2018: 181). Contrary to this perspective, if we assume that World Literature inevitably uses translation, recognizing English as a modern lingua franca seems not to be an obvious statement. The advantage of this language would therefore be that it does not require translation. This is, however, the false assumption that knowledge of a foreign language (and thus the ability to read a novel in that language) means no need for translation. Rather, I would say that it means an individualized, privatized, and often amateur translation. Therefore it requires supplementary effort and interpretative work from a non-English-native-speaker. One which typically should be covered to some extent by a publisher and a translator.

order to deconstruct the still binding cultural and literary hierarchies, it is not enough to add more volumes to an anthology or even "the" anthology if we take into account the status of the *Norton Anthology* (McInturff, 2003: 224-236; Hassan, 2000: 38-47). But most of all, we should probably include other ways of conceptualization than the next variants of the canon and subordinate canons (Damrosch, 2006: 43-53). I will risk expressing it directly: the realization of the project of World Literature as a non-hegemonic, global literary project requires not only a re-evaluation (and thus assigning value to previously devalued poetics, histories, individuals, communities) but also a new process of evaluation of literary pieces published every day. By turning to a ritual of non-judgment of contemporary works, we consciously slow down the process of dehegemonization. If we engage in the World Literature project with commitment, we must start looking for an evaluative language that does not resemble Buñuel's rubber poultry. Otherwise, we will inevitably find ourselves sitting alone under the table, secretly gorging on the forbidden fruit.

Works cited

Apter, Emily. *Against World Literature. On the Politics of Untranslatability*. London: Verso, 2013.

Belsey, Catherine. *Critical Practice*. Abingdon: Routledge, 1980.

Bhabha, Homi. "The World and the Home." *Social Text*, 31/32 (1992): 141-153.

Błoński, Jan. *Odmarsz. Wydawnictwo Literackie*. Kraków: Wydawnictwo Literackie, 1978.

Bolecki Włodzimierz, Tomasz Burek, Jerzy Jarzębski, Michał Paweł Markowski, Marian Stala, Marta Wyka. "Znikające cele krytyki?" In Tomasz Cieślak-Sokołowski and Dorota Kozicka (eds.), *Dyskursy krytyczne u progu XXI wieku. Między Rynkiem a uniwersytetem*. Kraków: TAiWPN Universitas, 2007: 410-446

Cieślak-Sokołowski, Tomasz. "Bieguny krytyki? Inspiracje metodologiczne polskiej krytyki literackiej u progu XXI wieku." In Tomasz Cieślak-Sokołowski and Dorota Kozicka (eds.), *Dyskursy krytyczne u progu XXI wieku. Między Rynkiem a uniwersytetem*. Kraków: TAiWPN Universitas, 2007: 377-391.

Cieślik, Krzysztof. "Krytyk musi umrzeć." *Dwutygodnik*, 182/2016, https://www.dwutygodnik.com/artykul/6475-krytyk-musi-umrzec.html

Damrosch, David. "World Literature in a Postcanonical, Hypercanonical Age." In Haun Saussy (ed.), *Comparative Literature in an Age of Globalization*. Baltimore: John Hopkins University Press, 2006: 43-53.

Danner, Mark and Robert Silvers. "In Conversation: Robert Silvers." *New York*, 05.04.2013, https://nymag.com/news/features/robert-silvers-2013-4/?mid=longreads

Eagleton, Terry. *The Function of Criticism* [1984]. London, New York: Verso, 2005.

Felski, Rita. *The Limits of Critique*. Chicago: University of Chicago Press, 2015.

Fisher, John. "Evaluation without Enjoyment." *The Journal of Aesthetics and Art Criticism*, 27/2 (1968): 135-139.

Gołuch, Dorota. "Polsko-postkolonialne podobieństwa? Recepcja tłumaczonej literatury postkolonialnej w Polsce (1970-2010)." *Przekładaniec*, 33 (2016): 46-70.

Hardwick, Elizabeth. "The Decline of Book Reviewing." *Harper's Magazine* (October 1959), [archive] https://harpers.org/archive/1959/10/the-decline-of-book-reviewing/

Hassan, Waïl S. "World Literature in the Age of Globalization: Reflections on an Anthology." *College English*, 63/1 (2000): 38-47

Hohendahl, Peter Uwe. *The Institution of Criticism* [1982]. Ithaca: Cornell University Press, 2016.

Hohendahl, Peter Uwe. "The Use Value of Contemporary and Future Literary Criticism." *New German Critique*, 7 (1976).

Jakubowiak, Maciej. "Pokłóćmy się o literature." *Dwutygodnik*, 181/2016, https://www.dwutygodnik.com/artykul/6458-poklocmy-sie-o-literature.html

Jakubowski, Jan Zygmunt (ed.). *Polska krytyka literacka (1800-1918). Materiały*. Warszawa: Państwowe Wydawnictwo Naukowe, 1959.

Jakubowski, Jan Zygmunt (ed.). *Polska krytyka literacka (1919-1939). Materiały*, red. J. Z. Jakubowski. Warszawa: Państwowe Wydawnictwo Naukowe, 1966.

Kowalcze-Pawlik, Anna. "Uwolnić Charybdę, pokochać Skyllę: o potworności przekładu." *Przekładaniec*, 24 (2011): 187-199.

Kraskowska, Ewa. "Porównywanie jako metoda krytyki przekładu." *Tekstualia*, 3/54 (2018): 53-62.

Larman Alexander, A Radical Proposal: Book reviews should review books, "The Critic", 12.05.2020, https://thecritic.co.uk/a-radical-proposal-book-reviews-should-review-books/

Longxi, Zhang. "World Literature, Canon, and Literary Criticism." In Fang Weigui (ed.), *Tensions in World Literature. Between the Local and the Universal*, London: Palgrave Macmillan, 2018: 171-190.

McInturff, Kate. "The Uses and Abuses of World Literature." *The Journal of American Culture*, 26/2 (2003): 224-236.

Mendelsohn, Daniel. "A Critic's Manifesto." *The New Yorker*, 28.08.2012, https://www.newyorker.com/books/page-turner/a-critics-manifesto

Mora Catlett, Juan Roberto. "Buñuel, the Realist: Variations of a Dream." In Kinder, Marsha (ed.), *Luis Buñuel's The Discreet Charm of the Bourgeoisie*. Cambridge: Cambridge University Press, 1999: 41-59.

Orliński, Marcin. "Nie bójmy się spierać." *Biblioteka. Magazyn Literacki* (2016), https://www.biuroliterackie.pl/biblioteka/debaty/nie-bojmy-sie-spierac/

Reiss, Katharina. *Translation Criticism – the Potentials and Limitations. Categories and Criteria for Translation Quality Assessment*, trans. Erroll F. Rhodes, Abingdon: Routledge, 2000.

Robson, William Wallace, *The Definition of Literature and Other Essays*, Cambridge: Cambridge University Press, 1982.

Sławiński, Janusz (ed.). *Badania nad krytyką literacką. Seria I*, Wrocław: Zakład Narodowy im. Ossolińskich, 1974.

Sławiński, Janusz. "Za co powinniśmy kochać Jana Błońskiego?" *Teksty: teoria literatury, krytyka, interpretacja*, 4/46 (1979): 1-9.

Vendler, Helen and Henri Cole. "The Art of Criticism No. 3." *The Paris Review*, 141 (Winter 1996), https://www.theparisreview.org/interviews/1324/the-art-of-criticism-no-3-helen-vendler

Wellek, René. *A History of Modern Criticism 1750-1950*, vol. I-VIII. New Haven: Yale University Press, 1955-1992.

Wellek, René. *Concepts of Criticism*. New Haven: Yale University Press, 1963.

Part 3.
Mediating between Images and Wor(l)ds

The Transnational Reach and Interpretation-Shaping Power of Book Illustrations and Defoe's *Robinson Crusoe* in 1720[1]

Sandro Jung

Printed images, especially book illustrations, do not have the status they deserve in scholarly accounts of the transmission of knowledge as meaningful, interpretive media of reception and as interdiscursive systems of textual production. In comparative literary studies, they have traditionally played a largely insignificant role, notwithstanding the fact that they facilitate a kind of readerly access to literary works that is distinctly different from that provided — via the mechanisms of script literacy — through the typographically realized text. Book illustrations possess mobility in that they imprint versions of themselves on readers' memories. Illustrations as well as the designs on which they are based also physically travel and are appropriated opportunistically, as occasion offers. Their travels and their significance for the writing of the transnational publishing of literary editions have, however, remained areas of the transmission of textual knowledge that are still in need of systematic further investigation. In the context of comparative literary studies, empirical illustration studies focus on how illustrations of frequently illustrated works are generated in an environment of interdependence and interrelationality. They probe the provenance, uses, and adaptations, as well as interpretive practices, of book illustrations. They reveal acts of exchange and

---

[1] I am grateful to Fiona McIntosh-Varjabédian and Karl Zieger for inviting me to give a version of this essay as a plenary at the 8th Congress of the European Society for Comparative Literary Studies. The essay is a short version of a significantly expanded study that appeared as "Book Illustration and the Transnational Mediation of *Robinson Crusoe* in 1720" in *Philological Quarterly*, 99:2 (2020), 171-201.

responsiveness that are at the core of the reception of literary works across different national book-producing and book-consuming publics.

In the visual economy of competing illustrated editions of literary works, those editions which, because of their affordability, are most accessible to readers have the greatest impact on training visual literacy and shaping a particular understanding of the text that an extensive engagement with the illustrations facilitates. In the case of the five different editions of German translations of *Robinson Crusoe* published in the year 1720, readers encountered illustrated editions of the work as the default material iteration of the text, rather than as the exception. The flagging of the copperplates on the title pages of the different editions became a standard move on the part of booksellers that defined the hybrid material identity of the codex. Furnishing every edition of a translated work of fiction with a large number of plates was not an ordinary phenomenon at a time when German booksellers tended not to illustrate their editions. This fact should be highlighted in order to understand how important the illustrations were in the textual transmission process of *Robinson Crusoe*. Furthermore, the plates in these editions are understood as explanatory devices which offer readers guidance, helping them to make sense of Defoe's narrative of religious conversion and colonization.

In what follows I will chart a hitherto unwritten chapter in the reception history of *Robinson Crusoe* on the continent. The neglect that the early reception of Defoe's work, including its earliest continental translations and their illustrations, has experienced, is largely due to the alleged priority of English series of illustrations (Blewett), even though these series all post-date those published on the continent in 1720. Equally, and with the exception of Otto Deneke, scholars have not undertaken detailed bibliographical research on the numerous variants of editions, including their illustrations, and how they functioned as part of an archive of transmission that, in turn, affected the ways in which illustrators in Britain interpreted *Robinson Crusoe*. Lastly, scholars have not explored the strategies underpinning the material packaging of editions and how these editions relate to one another in the year 1720, the year that the work first appeared in Dutch, French, and German. In this essay I will highlight the intercultural dynamics of book production which shaped the visual casting and reception of Defoe's text for Dutch, French, and German readers. I shall focus especially on the German context and examine in what ways the illustrations included in German editions of the work codified, through their selection, prominent moments from the narrative. At the same time, I shall consider how these visualizations — retailed, as they were, simultaneously, in large numbers, and over a long period of time (more than forty years) — came to occupy a literary meaning in cultural memory that associated them with Defoe's bestseller. The illustrations thus possessed a generative power in that they framed and contained widespread textual knowledge but also stimulated, in turn, the production of illustrations (and textual narratives) that adopted motifs and structural devices popularized by these images.

Establishing a chronology of editions and printings of *Robinson Crusoe* can facilitate an understanding of the immense demand that must have existed for the work. Such a chronology also makes it possible to gain a sense of how many thousands of copies of Defoe's text circulated and were able — through the affective power of their illustrations — to shape readerly understanding. It is well known that four editions of the work, which appeared in two volumes, *The Life and Strange Surprising Adventures of Robinson Crusoe* and *The Farther Adventures of Robinson Crusoe*, were published by William Taylor in London between April and October 1719. The former volume, *The Life and Adventures*, featured the iconic frontispiece image, engraved by John Clark and John Pine, of the protagonist armed with two fowling pieces and a sword, the background depicting, on the left, a storm-swept sea and ship in distress and, on the right, a fortified habitation. The latter, *Farther Adventures*, boasted a map. It was the commercial success of the first volume which induced continental publishers to commission translations and illustrations to cater for readers in languages other than English, and it will be the first volume that this essay will focus on.

From an examination of the use and wear of the frontispiece engraving as reflected by the plate impressions accompanying different editions, it is evident that it became necessary early on in the publishing of illustrated editions of the work to replace the frontispiece with a reengraving of the original design of the protagonist. Assuming that more than 1000, sometimes even 2000, copies could be printed from a single plate, it is possible to get a sense of the large number of copies that were produced in Britain in 1719 alone. Consulting the Bowyer printing ledgers, Keith Maslen has unearthed that three editions of Defoe's work were printed in print runs of 1000 copies each (Maslen: 147), and these 3000 copies, in addition to the editions for which no print run information survives, had to be supplied with plates, which would have exceeded the capacity of even a handful of engravings of each illustration. Like the addition of any engraved image, the engraving (and subsequent re-cutting) of plates entailed extra cost as part of the production of the printed work, although the principal expense would have consisted in the paper used for printing. Intaglio engraving being a time-consuming process, it could also significantly delay the issuing of a publication, thereby hampering the immediate recovery of outlay. As Britain operated a centralized book production market at the beginning of the eighteenth century, there were as yet no provincial editions of *Robinson Crusoe* that challenged Taylor's copyright monopoly and the decisions he made regarding the text's illustrated iterations. Edition after edition reused the frontispiece engraving originally designed for the copyright holder, thereby minimizing the cost of production—but at the cost of not offering any visual narrative shaping readerly consumption of the text, as editions produced on the continent did.

When for the sixth London edition, "Adorned with Cuts," of 1722, Taylor included six additional engravings, these offered little visual complexity, avoiding, with three exceptions, the foregrounding of human action. Instead, the illustrator adopts as a central mode a maritime iconic repertoire that is absent from editions produced two years earlier in Amsterdam and Germany. Robinson is identifiable as an individual in only two plates: first, in an illustration that visualizes a moment following his escape from the Moors in Africa, where, in a boat with the young Xury, he shoots a lion; and second, once he has been shipwrecked on the desert island, in the illustration capturing Robinson on a raft, salvaging goods from the wreck of the ship. Despite the fact that the protagonist is not zoomed in on by the designer of the remaining illustrations, the captions, without exception, reference Robinson and therefore, at least associatively, assert his presence and agency in those illustrations in which he cannot be discerned as an individual. The remaining scenes selected for visualization are derived from the final third of the narrative and include the liberation of Friday from the cannibals as well as the arrival of the English ship at Crusoe's island and its subsequent recapture, after a mutiny, by the protagonist and the ship's captain. These plates specify Defoe's narrative as a particular kind of work. It is presented as a tale of adventure, including piracy, and does not contextualize the protagonist's religious conversion.

These early illustrations occupy a particular role in the reception history of the text. By the time the 1722 set of plates was produced, the success of *Robinson Crusoe* had been established. No authorized competing editions of the work were retailed so that, from a marketing point of view, it was not necessary to add illustrations to distinguish one edition from another. The reason for the commissioning of the illustrations will likely have been motivated by considerations of how the text could and would be read. The unnamed illustrator, in selecting specific scenes in preference to others, presented an official and authenticated – some readers may have considered it an authorially approved – reading of the work. In not restricting itself to the visualization of the religious conversion narrative, the series, too, retained broad appeal.

When *Robinson Crusoe* appeared in Amsterdam in 1720 in both a four-volume Dutch and a three-volume French translation, the latter by Justus van Effen and Thémiseul de Saint-Hyacinthe, the visual framing of the editions could not have been more different than that of the English editions Taylor had issued up to that point. Much more than Taylor's, these Dutch editions were of transcultural significance, since they fed a visual culture in the form of illustrative apparatuses included in editions that would shape the perception and uptake of the work in more than one nation. Where English editions had established a standard format consisting both of the Clark-Pine frontispiece and the map, the volumes of the French-language edition, which were published by L'Honoré & Chatelain,[2] were embellished by 12 full-page plates, in addition to Bernard Picart's frontispiece. Picart's plate gave Robinson Crusoe a new visual identity, one that was adopted by booksellers in Germany, Italy, the Netherlands, and Sweden. According to David Blewett, much more so than the Clark-Pine image, Picart's image "has the benefit of familiarity with the text. Crusoe's stockade is indicated not by a flimsy picket fence but is shown with the stakes that have sprouted into trees and the ladder that can be pulled up for security" (Blewett: 32). Whereas the frontispiece was synoptic, offering a visual characterization of *Robinson Crusoe*, the plates were focused on specific situations and moments of action. Although the series of illustrations was not engraved by Picart, on whose established reputation as an outstanding artisan in the field the frontispiece had capitalized, the plates provided readers with visualizations of the episodic, "outlining [...] a story with a definite moral and spiritual development" (*ibid.*: 32). In contrast to the edition of the French translation, the Dutch translation included 18 full-page illustrations and adapted the Picart frontispiece. Equipping a recent title with as many as 18 illustrations was unusual. The large number of plates the Dutch publishers, de Jansoons van Waesberge, commissioned do not relate to a previous set of illustrations. Rather than secondary illustrations, deriving from, reworking, or responding to existing series of illustrations and thus occupying a secondary place in the hierarchy of transmission, the designs for the Dutch-language edition of *Robinson Crusoe* are primary illustrations. The series offered the most comprehensive and complex visual rendering of the novel at the time. Its profusion of illustrative

---

[2] L'Honoré & Chatelain also published illustrated editions of other best-selling works such as Jean de la Fontaine's *Fables Choisies* (1722) and *Le Théâtre de P. Corneille* (1723). In addition, they were map publishers and thus would have worked closely with members of the engraving trade.

material centralized the images in the mixed-media economy of the printed book by encouraging readers to conceive of them as a sequence of concatenated episodes, events, and moments textually defined by means of descriptive captions through which knowledge of the work could be gleaned. In their concentration, they represented a visual anthology which traced the protagonist's situation, mindset at various moments, and development.

That these two profusely illustrated editions were produced in Amsterdam was no coincidence, for the city boasted a highly developed engraving industry that regularly produced illustrations for books—although the de Jansoons van Waesberge firm did not publish any other illustrated work of fiction. By contrast, at the beginning of the eighteenth century, the London book market was largely dependent on immigrant copper engravers from the Low Countries and France to train English craftsmen. Clark had, in fact, been a pupil of Picart's and helped to improve figure engraving in London.

The speed with which both a French and a Dutch translation were produced testifies to the demand that publishers foresaw for their editions. The outlay necessary to finance the inclusion of 12 or even more plates was significant and could potentially bankrupt a bookseller if copies did not sell quickly enough. The French-language edition was undoubtedly targeted at French and German readers, whereas the Dutch translation will have catered to readers in the Dutch republic. But there would have been cross-over markets as well, especially since the Dutch-language edition was also retailed in Leipzig. Also, as Bernhard Fabian has noted, at the beginning of the eighteenth century "the Dutch book-market, which was a large European market, included Germany as a matter of course. Books from England, on the other hand, were often not available in Germany" (Fabian: 47-48).

The impact of both illustrated editions, despite the targeting of a particular language-specific readership, was profound.[3] It is

---

[3] The plates for the edition of the French translation have occasionally been (briefly) considered. See Blewett: 31-33; Jung: 42-43. By contrast, the illustrations accompanying the Dutch translation of *Robinson Crusoe* have not been considered by scholars of Defoe or those of Dutch book illustration,

essential to understand the two ventures within the context of fierce competition among booksellers to publish translations of Defoe's work. Once these translations were available, they were speedily reprinted. In the absence of specific dates of publication, I have been able to determine a terminus ante quem for the publication of the first volume of the French translation, *La Vie et les Avantures Surprenantes*, of April 1720, about a year after the publication of the first London edition. The second volume of the French translation was published by October that year. A terminus ante quem of June 1720 can be assumed for the edition of *Het Leven en Gevallen van Robinson Crusoe*.[4] Even though the Dutch translation was published only two months after the first volume of the French one, it will have been in the making for much longer. It is furthermore likely that a workshop of engravers rather than a single artisan undertook the execution of the unsigned designs, and that both editions of the Dutch and French translations had their origin in 1719.[5] Independently of these projects, the first German translation was being produced by Ludwig Friedrich Vischer in Hamburg, a sea port with particularly established links with the London book trade. These editions and translations were consciously produced not only to respond to the growing popularity and marketability of the text but in response to one another. They thus created an enmeshed textual archive that promoted different language and visual versions of the text. These versions of the text were not necessarily based on the English original. At the same time, and

---

despite the fact that the series of plates is a remarkable series in the history of the Dutch illustrated book. In her study of Dutch literary book illustration of the eighteenth century, *De Illustratie van letterkundige Werken in de XVIIIe Eeuw: Bijdrage tot de Geschiedenis van het nederlandsche Boek* (Amsterdam: H. J. Paris, 1934), Eleonore de la Fountaine Verwey did not recognise the unusual nature of the edition of the Dutch translation. She characterised the illustration of such translated English bestsellers as Samuel Richardson's *Pamela* and Henry Fielding's *Tom Jones* as drawing on reprinting practices rather than as commissioning original designs.

[4] See *Maendelyke Uittreksels, of Boekzael der geleerde Werelt*, 10 (1720): 501 and 508. See also W.H. Staverman: 34-37.

[5] The French translation was announced in *L'Europe Savante*, 11 (1719): 151, "*L'Honoré & Chatelain* impriment et donneront dans peu: *La Vie & les Avantures de Robinson Crusoe*: traduit de l'anglois."

with the exception of the first Hamburg edition of *Robinson Crusoe* in German, the illustrations that made the text present to Dutch, French, and German readers were not based on the English illustrations Taylor commissioned. Rather they reused a visual corpus conceived in Amsterdam and subsequently exported to Germany to mediate the English text. It was thus booksellers and artisans working in Amsterdam who shaped the visual narrative that readers encountered on the continent, although these illustrations were not adapted for use in any British edition of *Robinson Crusoe*.

The six full-page plates included in the first volume of the French translation offered the first ever visual narrative of Robinson's history. The unsigned engravings from the Dutch translation, termed on the title page of the edition merely "Figuren," only in three instances adopt the same subjects for illustration that had already occurred in the edition of the French translation, so there is little overlap in terms of subject matter represented. The three subjects shared by illustrations of both the editions of the French and the Dutch translations include visual renderings of Robinson's dream, Friday's accepting Robinson as his master after his being saved from the savages, and—the subject for an illustration for *Farther Adventures*—the protagonist's destruction of the pagan idol, Cham-Chi-Thaungu. Focusing on just these three subjects, a reader would have encountered a visual casting of Crusoe as a God-fearing individual and as the defender of monotheism. Through the first illustration, readers would have been directed to comprehend his conversion narrative as the result of being the disobedient son from the beginning of the narrative; his suffering would have been explained as the direct effect of not heeding his father's warning. Since Crusoe not only functions as Friday's deliverer but, subsequently, also as his spiritual guide, the act of submission on the part of the savage is also an act of devotion, just as much as Robinson's destruction of the non-Christian idol is an act of devotion to his God in confirming the first and second commandments.

The different ways of representing the same three subjects is of interest in that the diverse realization in visual form reflects multifarious reading experience. Read within the context of the series produced for the Dutch and French illustrations, it is striking how differently each series opens. While the latter edition opens with a scene of filial disobedience, captioned "Robinson devant son Pere, qui lui predit toute sortes [sic] de malheurs," emphasizing Crusoe's shipwreck as (divine) punishment, the former, Dutch edition's illustrations do not introduce familial concerns. It is the fourth illustration only which introduces the dream, albeit in a way that does not iconically reference scripture. The plate is captioned "Vervaarelyke Droom von R: Crusoe," the fear-inspiring dream, and captures a delirious vision induced by the consumption of tobacco soaked in rum in which the protagonist encounters an avenging angel: "he mov'd towards me, with a long spear or weapon in his hand, to kill me; and when he came to a rising ground, at some distance he spoke to me, or I heard a voice so terrible, that it is impossible to express the terror of it; all that I can say I understood was this, *Seeing all these things have not brought thee to repentance, now thou shalt die.* At which words, I thought he lifted up the spear that was in his hand to kill me."[6] The illustrator zooms in on the sublime encounter between the angel and Robinson but does not introduce the conversion moment that results from serious illness of which this delirious vision is a part. By contrast, the illustrator of the French translation had brought the two idea complexes together, representing the angel with spear and Robinson in a thought bubble above the protagonist, whereas the protagonist is shown recovered through the reading of the Bible. Although these two moments are temporally distinct, they are brought together by the designer who introduces the moment of anagnorisis in which Robinson, still ill and "too much disturb'd with the tobacco" (75), opened the Bible and "the first words that occurr'd to [him]" were "*Call on me in the day of trouble, and I will deliver, and thou shalt glorify me*" (75). The illustrator identifies the book Robinson is reading unmistakably by reproducing the text in

---

[6] Daniel Defoe, *Robinson Crusoe*, ed. with an introduction by John Richetti (London: Penguin, 1992), 70-71. All quotations are from this edition and supplied parenthetically in the text.

French, "Invoque moi au jour de ton affliction et je te delivrerai" (Figures 1a and 1b).

When the plate from the French edition was adapted for use in Germany, the text on the open book in the fourth edition of the text, issued by the Leipzig publisher, Johann Christian Martini, was translated, "Ruf mich an in der Noth so will ich dich erretten." However, not every German edition of *Robinson Crusoe* published in 1720-21 possessed an exact copy of the plate, the Leipzig edition issued by Weidmann in 1720 not reproducing the writing on the book—probably to save the engraving cost or out of the conviction that attentive readers would have been able to identify the book represented and its role in the conversion of Robinson.

Despite the different ways of engaging with the subject of Robinson's dream, the illustrators for the Amsterdam editions of the Dutch and French translations realized the significance this moment had for the development of Robinson's character and the acknowledgment of Providence in the narrative as a whole. The three illustrations that follow the visualization of Robinson's dream in the edition of the Dutch translation cast him as creator, recreating European material culture and its conveniences on the island. He is shown as an architect constructing his habitation, as a potter capable of preserving and storing his food items, as a shipbuilder, producing a canoe, and as a tailor making his own clothes. Whereas he still overreaches himself in the building of his canoe, constructing a vessel which, due to its weight, he is unable to transport to the sea, each effort to recreate civilization is followed by thanksgiving and prayer, and he is able to live contentedly and resigned to the will of God.

The final subject that both the illustrator for the edition of the French translation and that for the Dutch translation adopted was the saving of Friday from the savages who were preparing to sacrifice and devour him. The illustrator for the former edition presents Man Friday in the process of kneeling but not before he has severed the head of his persecutor, which he presents to Robinson and which is lying on the ground, next to the protagonist's sword. The design for the latter edition captures a different moment, which subsequently was widely adopted for illustrations in the English-speaking world. The scene is realized in a more sanitized manner (Figures 2a and 2b). No beheaded bodies are on view. Instead, Friday is shown in an act of proskynesis, as described by the narrator: he "kiss'd the ground, and laid his head upon the ground, and taking me by the foot, set my foot upon his head; this, it seems, was in token of swearing to be my slave for ever" (161). Both images represent Robinson as father figure— signaled through the admonishing finger and the benevolent facial expression. He is in the process of accepting Friday into his care and will in due course use Friday as a medium of religious, spiritual, and moral instruction for both the savage and himself.

The series of plates in the edition of the Dutch-language translation concludes with Crusoe's return to his native country. It thus promotes an holistic understanding of the novel that covers its entirety, including the liberation of Friday, the charity towards the Spaniard, and Robinson's saving of the captain. As a result, the series, which illustrated Crusoe's pre-island existence in two plates only, charts the effects of his shipwreck, his conversion, and his eventual salvation. After his dream, he embraces the will of God and finds deliverance in accepting his lot on the island but finally, through the grace of the Lord, is removed from it.

In the same year that the French and Dutch translations were published in Amsterdam, five illustrated editions of German translations of *Robinson Crusoe*—some based on the English original, others on the French text—were published in Hamburg and Leipzig, two major centres of book production. From 1727, further editions were published by the Felßecker firm in Nuremberg who would retain the monopoly to republish editions of Defoe's novels for 51 years. Otto Deneke has provided the most comprehensive study of the genealogy of these editions as well as their relationships to one another. He did not pay sufficient attention to the illustrations, including questions of their provenance, however. The first German translation was published by the Hamburg firm of the heirs of Thomas Wiering in April 1720 (Deneke: 3-5), the translator's preface being dated 26 March 1720. It reprinted the Clark-Pine frontispiece, which was executed by the Hamburg engraver, Christian Fritzsch, but which is qualitatively inferior to the English original. In November, at the earliest, Wiering's Leipzig competitor, Moritz Georg Weidmann, published in "Franckfurth and Leipzig" an edition of his own, the fifth to be published in 1720, which did not reuse the frontispiece the Hamburg edition had used (Deneke: 15-16). Instead, he reprinted the illustrations that accompanied the first volume of the French translation published in Amsterdam earlier that year. Since German publishers of *Robinson Crusoe* followed their Dutch peers' practice and published volume by volume, rather than issuing a multiple-volume edition simultaneously, Weidmann's reprinting the illustrations that had only recently been issued in Amsterdam reflects very recent knowledge of the French-language edition. Only in a book production centre such as Leipzig was it possible to bring together different agents of print to produce an illustrated edition of the work in such a short period of time. Whereas Wiering had undertaken his edition when the French translation had not yet been published and its illustrations not yet been available, his cost-saving practice stood out once later German editions appeared that went beyond the inclusion of the portrait frontispiece and the map. His edition set off a chain reaction among booksellers in Germany, which resulted in the centralizing of the illustrations in a manner that codified the illustrated edition as the appropriate format for editions of *Robinson Crusoe*. Wiering was the first to complete the race for publishing an illustrated German translation, at a time when, through existing book-trade connections and the increasing number of translated excerpts from *Robinson Crusoe* published in the German and Dutch periodical press at the time, he would have been apprised of ventures to cater to continental demand for what was quickly turning into a staple of popular literature.

Although only the name of the Leipzig publisher, Martini, is given on the title page of the fourth German edition of Defoe's novel, *Das Leben und die gantz ungemeine Begebenheiten des Robinson Crusoe*, the preface of which was dated July 1720, he had, in fact, reprinted—with some changes and the anonymous title page publishing imprint "Franckfurth und Leipzig"—the text that Wiering had commissioned for his edition (Deneke: 5-15). He supplied purchasers of his volume with twelve plates and a map, and further helped readers to make sense of the visual apparatus by furnishing an explanation of the first plate, which depicted Robinson Crusoe and his father. Martini thus glossed the meaning of the plate, thereby encouraging his readers to read the illustrations as textual commentary. Rather than explicating the subject of the plate as other engravers had done through the addition of a caption, as in the fifth edition, "Robinson stehet vor seinem Vater, der ihm alle sein Unglück vorher saget," Martini in the Preface to the edition recasts the plate as a capturing of the protagonist's innocence on departing from England: "Vorgesetztes Kupffer-Blatt stellet dir den Welt-beruffenen Robinson Crusoe in neuen Unternehmungen und wunderlichen Begebenheiten zum andern. Er ist noch nicht ermüdet, den Lesern zu erbaulichen Zeit-Vertreib oder unschuldigen Ergötzen [...] von seinen ferner merckwürdigen Reisen und Schicksalen aufrichtig mitzutheilen."

Martini had published the first volume of his edition by September 1720.[7] The second followed within a month, by which time the bookseller advertised that, provided they purchased his second volume, buyers whose copies of the first volume did not contain the six illustrations of his first volume would be furnished with a set of the plates free of charge.[8] While this was primarily aimed at those who had purchased Wiering's edition, it is also likely that editions were sold, at a lower price, without plates and that sets of the engravings could be purchased separately. Although geographically remote from Leipzig, the Hamburg Wiering firm had, through their agent and Leipzig Book Fair representative, Philip Hertel, supplied the Leipzig book market with its edition of *Robinson Crusoe* so that potential purchasers would have been able to choose from the four editions published up to October 1720. Martini's offer of a free set of six plates was enticing as well as an excellent marketing ploy. Having access to four different editions that were all on sale in Leipzig gave readers a choice to select the edition they wanted to purchase but also the

---

[7] See *Neue Zeitungen von Gelehrten Sachen auf das Jahr 1720* (Leipzig: in der Zeitungs-Expedition, 1720): 576.
[8] *Ibid.*: 654.

opportunity to familiarize themselves with the illustrative apparatus of each edition, as these were central to the editions' brand identity. In a review of Martini's edition, the plates received commendation for bringing to life the protagonist's adventures.[9]

Martini adopted a visual apparatus that differed from the one that Weidmann would subsequently copy from the Amsterdam edition of the French translation. For this edition, a new illustrative apparatus was adopted. The series he had engraved for his editions have led to confusion among the two scholars who have written about them. Deneke, examining copies now lost, records variants of the plates that were signed by the Leipzig engravers, J. B. Brühl and J. G. Krüger, while also encountering the same designs where the plates do not carry the names of the engravers. He maintains that Brühl is likely to have been responsible for these supposedly original designs (Deneke: 12). Bethany Wiggin, the only recent scholar to have studied the eighteenth-century German reception of *Robinson Crusoe*, does not appear to be aware of Deneke's ground-breaking bibliographical work and misidentifies Martini's "Franckfurth and Leipzig" edition as having been published by Weidmann. Like Deneke, she records that the publisher "outfitted his *Crusoe* with twelve plates, six of which I have not been able to locate in any other English, French, or Dutch edition" (Wiggin: 198). She implicitly acknowledges the six plates as newly commissioned, observing that the edition's "many fashionable plates emphasized its novel appeal" (*ibid.*: 199). Deneke and Wiggin are both wrong about the original status of the illustrations, for the six images Wiggin was unable "to locate" are, in fact, adaptations of existing plates, specifically the set of plates that appeared in the Amsterdam edition of the Dutch translation (Figures 3a and 3b). In the first place, these adaptations are less expertly engraved than the originals, and in two instances they redact the original designs, in the process altering the imagological identity of the protagonist. Martini adopted the plates captioned "Crusoe ontflaat zich van de Moor, en vlugt," "Crusoe begint een Logement te vervaerdigen," "Crusoe maakt potten tot zyn provisie," and "Crusoe bereydt zich

---

[9] *Neue Zeitungen von Gelehrten Sachen auf das Jahr 1720*: 654, "Die vielen beygefügten Kupfer stellen die vornehmsten Begebenheiten recht lebhafft dar."

Kleedren" but had the designs of the second and third illustrations altered. His plates captioned "Robinson will sich eine Wohnung machen" and "Robinson macht große Toepffe zu seinem Proviant" differ in terms of quality and tonality from the Dutch models; and, apart from the clumsily rendered body of the protagonist, they feature Robinson with a hat that he is not wearing in the originals. In terms of adapting existing illustrations, such a specific addition is highly unusual, especially since the remainder of the composition is retained and copied accurately. The hat, therefore, likely possesses particular imagological significance. Alternatively, the decision to introduce it reflects an attempt on the part of the publisher to authenticate the protagonist in the way Picart's more accurate rendering of Robinson Crusoe in his frontispiece did. In other words, the addition of the hat may have been an effort on the part of the German publisher to synchronize the image with the text where Robinson's hat is mentioned as one of the characteristics of his physical appearance.

Martini's illustrative apparatus reveals his familiarity with both Amsterdam editions. His decision to combine images selected from both editions with a view to creating an effect of novelty testifies to the fact that book buyers paid particular attention to the illustrations and that they would, as a result, have recognized that the editions issued by Martini and Weidmann differed both from Wiering's and from one another. They would likely not have been able to confirm the provenance of the illustrations from the Dutch translation—the origin of the French translation illustrations being acknowledged in book reviews at the time. But these illustrations stood out from all others featuring in German editions of Defoe's work through their extending the visual repertoire of iconic interpretation by representing scenes that had not been illustrated in the edition of the French translation.

While at the time of their publication in Amsterdam, the editions of the Dutch and French translations would have operated within a reading economy where readers may have encountered both sets of illustrated volumes in bookshops, they still offered readers two separate visual-interpretive sequences with and through which to understand Defoe's text. Each of these was contained by the physical form of the codex. Once Martini decided to select an equal number from each of the Amsterdam editions to create a composite illustrative apparatus, however, the threshold of difference and distinction was removed in favor of a sequence that altered the aggregate meanings of the new series. As a result, the relational reading of these illustrations differed from the respective readings of each series on its own—especially when compared to Weidmann's reuse of the series accompanying the edition of the French translation.

From its initial publication 300 years ago in London, *Robinson Crusoe* appeared framed by illustrations. Taylor's two illustrations, especially the Clark-Pine frontispiece, started an engagement on the part of visual interpreters of the work that was decisively developed not in Britain, but in Amsterdam. Both publishers of the editions of the French and Dutch translations must have been assured of the commercial success of the volumes they were issuing to invest heavily in the production of their series of plates. As the first two sequences of illustrations of the text, they are records of how readers—the artisan-readers instructed to translate the text into the medium of the illustration—responded to the text. That these illustrations were then adopted by German publishers of no fewer than five editions published in a single year is partly to be explained by the fact that the decentralized book market of Germany at the time had not as yet developed an illustration culture for new fiction; as a result, the reprinting of image material from abroad became popular. The manner of the adoption of *Robinson Crusoe* into Germany is unique, however, in that publishers not merely had the illustrations reprinted but in the case of the Martini editions had them redacted. The German uptake of *Robinson Crusoe* and the Dutch illustrations is more than an opportunistic cashing in on a popular media commodity, and the charting of this particular early chapter in the reception of Defoe's classic therefore reveals the dynamics of textual, including iconotextual, engagement that was to develop in greater complexity in the second half of the eighteenth century. Not recognizing that the British visual history of Defoe's classic owes much to the Dutch illustrations and their popularization in German editions is to misunderstand the truly international appeal that *Robinson Crusoe* had within months of its first publication.

Figure 1a: "Vervaarelyke Droom van R: Crusoe," *Het Leven en de wonderbare Gevallen van Robinson Crusoe* (Amsterdam, 1721). Courtesy Beinecke Rare Book and Manuscript Library, Yale University (call mark: Defoe 53 p721b).

Figure 1b: "Réve et Conversion de Robinson," *La Vie et les Avantures Surprenantes de Robinson Crusoe* (Amsterdam, 1720). Reproduced from a copy in the author's collection.

Figure 2a: "Le Sauvage apres sa delivrance se posterne aux pieds de Robinson," *La Vie et les Avantures Surprenantes de Robinson Crusoe* (Amsterdam, 1720). Reproduced from a copy in the author's collection.

Le Sauvage apres sa delivrance se prosterne aux pieds de Robinson.

Figure 2b: "Een Cannibaal onderwerpt zich aan Crusoe," *Het Leven en de wonderbare Gevallen van Robinson Crusoe* (Amsterdam, 1721). Courtesy Beinecke Rare Book and Manuscript Library, Yale University (call mark: Defoe 53 p721b).

Figure 3a: "Crusoe begint een Logement te vervaardigen," *Het Leven en de wonderbare Gevallen van Robinson Crusoe* (Amsterdam, 1721). Courtesy Beinecke Rare Book and Manuscript Library, Yale University (call mark: Defoe 53 p721b).

Figure 3b: "Robinson will sich eine Wohnung machen," *Das Leben und die gantz ungemeine Begebenheiten des Robinson Crusoe* (Frankfurt/ Leipzig, 1720). Reproduced from a copy in the author's collection.

References

Blewett, David. *The Illustration of "Robinson Crusoe," 1719-1920*. Gerrards Cross: Colin Smythe, 1995.

Deneke, Otto. *"Robinson Crusoe" in Deutschland: Die Frühdrucke, 1720-1780*. Göttingen: beim Herausgeber [der Göttingische Nebenstunden], 1934.

Fabian, Bernhard. *The English Book in Eighteenth-Century Germany*. London: The British Library, 1992.

Fountaine Verwey, Eleonore de la. *De Illustratie van letterkundige Werken in de XVIIIe Eeuw: Bijdrage tot de Geschiedenis van het nederlandsche Boek*. Amsterdam: H. J. Paris, 1934.

Jung, Sandro. *Kleine artige Kupfer: Buchillustration im 18. Jahrhundert*. Wiesbaden: Harrassowitz, 2018.

Maslen, Keith. "Edition Quantities for *Robinson Crusoe*, 1719." *The Library*, 24 (1969): 147.

Staverman, W.H. *"Robinson Crusoe" in Nederland: Een Bijdrage tot de Geschiedenis van den Roman in de XVIIIe Eeuw*. Groningen: DeWaal, 1907.

Wiggin, Bethany. *Novel Translations: The European Novel and the German Book, 1680-1730*. Ithaca, New York: Cornell University Press, 2011.

The Transmission of Knowledge in European Adventure Fiction of the Amazon

Jobst Welge (Universität Leipzig)

During the 19th and 20th century the cultural response to tropical nature, as exemplified by the Amazon region, and as expressed by both European and American travellers, scientists, and authors, became increasingly pre-conditioned by the cultural transmission and circulation of knowledge. With regard to European fictions of the Amazon, the rainforest was conceived as a redeployment of colonial tropes of discovery and exploration, in a border region between nature and culture, an almost metaphysical realm outside of time and space. A quest or travel narrative is typically organized around the ambivalence between the attraction to an original source, often figured according to the myth of Eldorado and its promise of material riches, and the repulsion felt towards barbarian, pre-civilized forces. Therefore, the cultural construction of the Amazon region is from the beginning shaped by an external, European, international perspective that requires a comparative approach (Pizarro, Rogers, Welge).

Furthermore, it is not surprising that, toward the end of the nineteenth century, this conjunction of tropes and discourses should also enter the genre of the adventure novel. In the following, I would like to look at two instances of such tropical adventure novels set in the Brazilian Amazon region: Jules Verne's novel *La Jangada. Huit cents lieues sur l'Amazone* (1881) and Arthur Conan Doyle's *The Lost World* (1912). Significantly, both novels are based on a travel plot that doubles as the reader's introduction into a realm of cultural and natural otherness. Another obvious commonality between the two works is the fact that their fictional adventure plots are combined with the representation of geographic and scientific knowledge that is not based on first-hand travel experience of their respective authors: neither Verne nor Doyle have ever been to the Amazon. In the following, I want to show what sort of epistemological discourses are redeployed through these popular novels. As I will argue, the question of how the relation between nature and culture is represented reflects contemporary ideas of temporality and evolution. Moreover, in the novels, knowledge formation is self-consciously linked to procedures of reading and detection, as well as to the relation between truth and fiction.

Travel, Civilization, and Knowledge in Verne's *La Jangada*

As almost always in Verne's novels, *La Jangada. Huit cents lieues sur l'Amazone* is also conceived along the route of a travel. Specifically, the work combines the scheme of the travel novel with the notion of a quest, as well as the idea of an enigma to be solved (Wolfzettel: 67). The novel's narrative begins in Peru, during the year 1852. The rich plantation owner ("fazendeiro") João Garral constructs a giant raft—the *jangada* of the title—in order to travel with his entire family from Iquitos to Belém. The motif for the journey is the impending marriage of his daughter Minha with Manoel Valdez, the best friend of his son Benito, whose mother lives in Belém. However, a further reason for the river voyage is the clarification of a juridical case, namely the revision of a sentence through which, twenty-three years ago, Garral had falsely been accused of murder and of the theft of diamonds, during the time he had been working in the imperial mines of Vila Rica (today: Ouro Preto in Minas Gerais), and when he still bore his real name, João da Costa. Thereafter, he had fled from the Brazilian authorities over the Peruvian frontier to Iquitos, forever hiding these troubling events from his family. During the boat journey the traveling group meets Torres, a mysterious bush captain who asks for permission to accompany them to Belém. Knowing of Garral's/João's past, he tries to blackmail him, although he is aware of his innocence and in possession of an encrypted note that contains the name of the true thief and murderer.

First, it should be pointed out that in contrast to the typical scenario in other novels by Verne, *La Jangada* does not feature

European travellers exploring foreign regions, but instead we have Brazilian characters (of European descent) travelling through Brazil.[1] However, as we will see, the perception of landscape and native customs is still constructed as an "external" perspective, thus echoing the perspective of the European reader who likewise enters a foreign space. For the surprisingly detailed and often (if not always)[2] historically and geographically accurate representation of the Amazon region and elements of Brazilian culture Verne relied on the geographical and scientific works of numerous travel writers. At the time of writing, several scientific expeditions had been achieved, most notably those by Jean Louis Rodolphe Agassiz (1807-1873) and Paul Marcoy (1815-1887).[3] Again and again, the omniscient narrator explicitly refers to such scientific travelogues and their authors, which undoubtedly shows that the representation of exotic nature and foreign lands is extrapolated from bookish knowledge. For instance, in the course of the novel Verne refers directly to the writings of Alexander von Humboldt, namely with regard to the general possibilities of navigating the Amazon,[4] or to Auguste de Saint-Hilaire, Émile Carrey, Henry Walter Bates, and several others.[5] For *La Jangada*, Verne was also directly assisted by the geographer Gabriel Marcel, director of the Département Géographique of the Bibliothèque Nationale (Borges).

---

[1] This circumstance is somewhat misrepresented by Roberto González Echevarría: 234.
[2] See, for instance, the following observation on Verne's geographical knowledge in Patrick Deville's *Amazonia* (2019), a text that is as much novel and travel literature as an essayistic reflection about prior Amazonian texts: "Sa géographie du nord péruvien est celle de l'époque, un peu approximative, même fautive dans ses exposés didactiques […]" (Deville: 172).
[3] On these and other scientific explorers, see Souza: 163-165, Rogers: 32-34.
[4] See, for instance, "Notice d'un voyage aux tropiques, exécuté par MM. Humboldt et Bonpland, par J.-C. Delamétherie" (1804), in Alexander von Humboldt, *Sämtliche Schriften*, vol. II, 1800-1809, edited by Sarah Bärtschi and Rex Clark, München: dtv, 2019, 242-252.
[5] Émile Carrey, *L'Amazone: Huit jours sous l'Équateur*, Paris: M. Lévy frères, 1856; Auguste de Saint-Hilaire, *Voyage dans le district des diamans et sur le littoral du Brésil*, Paris: Librairie-Gide, 1833; Henry Walter Bates, *The Naturalist on the River Amazon, A Record of Adventures, Habits of Animals, Sketches of Brazilian and Indian Life, and Aspects of Nature Under the Equator, During Eleven Years of Travel*, London: John Murray, 1863. The title makes abundantly clear that scientific and adventure writing were not seen as distinct during this period.

La Jangada, then, was part of the collection *Voyages Extraordinaires*, created by Pierre-Jules Hetzel, which intended to publish "the whole world as a novel, setting each adventure in a different part of the planet" (Borges: 497)[6]. As Mariano Siskind has recently argued, the literature of Verne provides a productive case study for what he calls "the novelization of the globe," arguing that Verne's novels should not merely be understood as expressing the ideology of European colonialism, but as "some of the most radical imaginaries of the transformation of the planet into a totality of modern culture and sociability," voicing a limitless "dream of universal economic and political freedom" (Siskind: 39-40), a global project which could not possibly be entrusted to one single novel. At the same time, Siskind shows, Verne's literary production also participates in what he calls "the globalization of the novel," as his works reach a vast, international, transatlantic readership. Thus, the French publishing house Garnier was established in 1844 in Rio de Janeiro to foster the distribution of French imported books, and in fact, in the very year of its publication *La Jangada* reached an — admittedly very small — Brazilian readership.[7] In the context of the novel's broad intertextual basis, it is highly significant that before the beginning of the voyage, Garral's daughter Minha is eager to consult books on the Amazon. The books in the library function as a conduit for the link between bookish knowledge and direct visual observation:

> Allons à la bibliothèque, dit-elle! Prenons tous les livres, toutes les cartes qui peuvent nous faire connaître ce bassin magnifique! Il ne s'agit pas de voyager en aveugles! Je veux tout voir de ce roi des fleuves de la terre! (Verne: 36)

The promotion of knowledge certainly stresses the economic potential of the Amazon as a source and a venue for trade. Aside from the enormous biodiversity and the gigantic extension of the Amazon, the novel stresses its moderate climate, which thus provides good conditions for mercantile use (Verne: 89).

---

[6] All translations, unless otherwise indicated, are my own.
[7] For a study of the market of French books in Brazil, see Abreu: 15-38.

Yet, even as the travellers re-enact the course of historic colonial and scientific explorers, the narrative repeatedly stresses the purely aesthetic potential of the landscape and the river: "Fleuve incomparable, en vérité! répondit Manoel, et j'en comprends toutes les sublimes beautés! Nous le descendons, maintenant, comme Orellana, comme La Condamine l'ont fait, il y a des siècles, et je ne m'étonne plus qu'ils en aient rapporté de si merveilleuses descriptions!" (Verne, 98).[8] The giant raft ("jangada") on which the voyage is undertaken, with its provisions of livestock, housings for the Black and Indio workers, is generally presented as a reproduction of the home left behind, a complete version of a master's house (a "fazenda"), a swimming garden ("jardin flottant"), a comfortable island of civilization within a tropical scenery that is not very threatening—and where cannibalism and barbarity are said to be only a myth of bygone times. This idea of a shielded, protected island as a means of transformation is, of course, a recurring motif in the adventure fiction of Jules Verne (*L'île mystérieuse*; *Vingt mille lieues sous les mers*). Yet the raft is not entirely separate from its natural surroundings; rather, it is a symbol for the combination of nature and culture (as when the family house is lushly decorated with lianas and bromelias).

This garden-like decoration of the housing is carried out by Minha, Lina (her mulatto maid), as well as Fragoso, who had been saved from suicide by Lina's spontaneous pursuit of the course of a liana (ch. 7: "en suivant une liane"). The liana will eventually unite Lina and Fragoso (ch. 7: "un lien entre nous"), and at the end of the novel Fragoso will state in fact the symbolic identity between Lina and the liana. The mystery plot, just as the orientation in the disordered jungle, will be brought toward a restoration of order. The pursuit of the liana, then, is described as the "Ariadne thread" through a labyrinth, as a "fil conducteur" (Verne: 61), a metaphorics of orientation echoed by the river voyage itself.[9] A later scene has

---

[8] On Orellana, see Pizarro: 72-75; Rogers: 73-74.

[9] "Une liane gigantesque reliait entre eux tous ces parasites; elle faisait plusieurs fois le tour de la maison, elle s'accrochait à tous les angles, elle s'enguirlandait à toutes les saillies, elle se bifurquait, elle 'touffait,' elle jetait à tort et à travers ses fantaisistes ramicelles, elle ne laissait plus rien voir de l'habitation, qui

the forest float in front of the raft as in a mobile panorama. The halting of the narrative progression in visual, scenic tableaux and their effect of "making present" is in fact a general feature of Verne's novels (Dünne: 68).

The female characters Minha and Lina may be said to belong to the realm of botany, and Minha, whenever possible, deters her brother and her fiancé Manoel from hunting animals, thus embodying the non-utilitarian principle of contemplating, not killing nature. While the principal, patriarchal character is certainly innocent in terms of juridical justice, his role as archetypal "civilizer" of the land implies that the construction of the *jangada*, as a technical feat and aesthetically adorned object, is the result of violence against nature:

> Peut-être quelques braves gens, peu habitués à ces *grands massacres d'arbres*, eussent-ils gémi en voyant des géants, qui comptaient plusieurs siècles d'existence, tomber [...]. Les vieux troncs dépouillèrent leurs vêtements de lianes, de cactus, de fougères, de mousses, de bromélias. Leur écorce se montra à nu, en attendant qu'ils fussent *écorchés vifs* à leur tour. (Verne: 47, emphasis mine)

At the end of the novel, order is re-established when Garral's son, Benito, kills Torres, and when the retrieved document is finally deciphered. In this sense, I would argue, Verne's novel, befitting his supportive stance vis-a-vis the state's *mission civilisatrice*, portrays the Amazon in light of a potential conflict between the aesthetic contemplation and the economic use of nature, a conflict that has already brought about certain losses — given that the plot is set in the past of 1852. In the light of previous topical discourses about the Amazon, *La Jangada* suggests a mostly benign and harmless vision of nature, where formerly savage Indians have been largely tamed; with the exception of an attack by crocodiles (ch. 17), an electric eel, and the threat of giant snakes. The novel shows us a highly visual representation of nature, which is at the same time marked as eminently textual, namely by the rhetoric of "decipherment," as

---

semblait être enfouie sous un énorme buisson en fleur. Attention délicate et dont on reconnaîtra aisément l'*auteur*, l'extrêmité de ce cipo allait s'épanouir à la fenêtre même de la jeune mulâtresse," Verne: 73; my emphasis.

well as by the explicit references to previous travelogues, both by the omniscient narrator and the characters themselves. The voyage along the Amazon is here, at least in terms of the clarification of the mystery plot, a voyage into the past. With hindsight, the present of narration points toward future developments that are welcomed in the name of progress, so that the present appears as a Romantic equilibrium, already in a nostalgic light. At the novel's end, the final voyage back occurs not with the raft, but with a steamboat. The era of modern transportation has begun.

Knowledge and Temporality: Conan Doyle's *The Lost World*

A voyage into a much more distant past and a more ambivalent view of modernity is enacted in Conan Doyle's *The Lost World*. This novel, through which the author sought to transfer his popular success with the detective novel towards adventure fiction, is clearly marked by the tradition of Jules Verne. In fact, both the novel and its characters may be described as composite formations of different models and sources (Stiegler: 126 ff; Duncan: x). The pattern of the quest romance is here motivated by the scientific challenge resulting from the fact that a British zoologist, the aptly named Professor Challenger, seeks to convince his contemporaries of the evidence of prehistoric dinosaurs having survived on an island plateau in the Amazon region. Challenger publicly solicits volunteers from a lecture hall: an English explorer, a fellow colleague, and an Irish reporter, Malone, who doubles also as the narrator of the novel. Challenger's discovery is said to have penetrated into regions neglected by his predecessors Henry Walter Bates and Alfred Russel Wallace, the two great Victorian traveller-scientists to have anticipated the Darwinian theory of evolution through their observations of animal species in the Amazon.

In the public debates at the beginning of the novel, the various professors agree as regards the single-minded progression of the species. The question of whether the interim species, or links, on the chain of life still exist, is emphatically advanced by Challenger. His basic assumption, namely that an earlier period of life has survived into the present, resonates with contemporary colonial assumptions about so-called primitive people, who are understood as a conservation of an earlier, pre-civilizational stage of humankind (Fabian). The novel also self-consciously acknowledges the fact that it enters somewhat belatedly into the genre of imperial fiction: "The big blank spaces in the map are all being filled in, and there's no room for romance anywhere" (Doyle: 10). This quote is in turn an echo of Joseph Conrad's *Heart of Darkness* (1899), where Marlow states early on: "At that time there were many blank spaces on the earth [...]" (Conrad: 33).

Significantly, the reader is drawn into this narrative through the perspective of a journalist whose function is twofold: first, to participate in the adventurous expedition as a proof of his own manliness, and secondly, to testify and report the truth of what he has witnessed. The journalistic world as a token of truth doubles in the form of the novel as narrated by Malone in the first person, since other forms of material evidence have been lost. The remote space of the Amazon plateau is countered by a scenery of London that contains the institutions of journalism and of a scientific community (ch. I-VI), in other words, two professions that rely heavily on a principle of intersubjective truth. The group of men, including Malone, who set out on the expedition that seeks to verify the earlier expedition of an American called Maple White, is engaged in taking notes, producing scrapbooks and photographs, thereby to provide consequential evidence for the London lecture hall audience in the last chapter of the novel. Most of the photographs are said to have been destroyed, and the few remaining ones produce sceptical reactions from the audience and the following rhetorical question by the narrator: "What did it amount to? Some photographs. Was it possible that in this age of ingenious manipulation photographs could be accepted as evidence?" (Doyle: 181)

Professor Challenger as well as the rest of the party of explorers had partial counterparts in the real world. Thus, Professor Summerlee was apparently based on Sir Robert Christison, a Scottish Professor of Medicine. The character of Lord John Roxton bears a resemblance to Roger Casement, a British consul who took an active role in trying to stop the atrocities that were taking place in the Belgian Congo and subsequently, when he was sent to the Brazilian Amazon, took a similar role for the defenseless native workers of a large rubber company.[10] Edward Malone's character might have been based on the French-born British reporter Edmund Dene Morel, who co-founded the Congo Reform Association with Casement.[11] The rhetoric of scientific proof and truth was ironically undercut by Arthur Conan Doyle when he had himself photographed in the guise of Professor Challenger, or when he staged composite photographs of the fictional members of the expedition (Stiegler: 128 ff).

There is no evidence that Doyle was aware of *La Jangada*, yet the general influence of Verne becomes clear via a certain resemblance with his much better-known work *Voyage au centre de la terre* (1864). First, there is the notion that a voyage to a remote region difficult to access amounts to a sort of travel to a pre-historic, geologically sedimented level of time that has been shielded from a subsequent temporal development—and thus serves as a sort of material and living archive of evolution (Dünne: 59 ff; Henrikson and Kullberg). Furthermore, the plots of the novels by Verne and Doyle are each motivated by the puzzle of a cryptogram (in the case of Verne, mediated by E. A. Poe's *The Gold-Bug*, 1843), which I take to point to a meta-epistemological scenario, namely the ways in which the novels foreground their own textuality and their "deciphering" stance versus nature or natural history (Doyle: 171).

Moreover, there is an analogy between the footprint of the dinosaurs as evidence of their presence, and the photograph as in turn an imprint of this image, as it was included in some editions of the novel (Stiegler: 129 ff). The novel thus explores what Carlo Ginzburg in a famous essay once called an indiciary paradigm, namely the attempt to decipher who or what has been present in a given site, thus providing an analogy between the hunter's reading of animal traces, psychoanalysis, and the diagnostic method of

---

[10] On Casement, see Uriarte. For a literary account of Casement's life, see also Mario Vargas Llosa's novel *El sueño del celta* (2010).

[11] Doyle was also involved with this circle, for which he wrote *The Crime of the Congo* (1909).

Doyle's Sherlock Holmes. This means that the trace as evidence constantly seems to bridge a living presence with the reconstruction in the face of its present absence. Yet, even the photographs that Challenger has brought back from his first expedition have been damaged, and he is subsequently accused of fraud. This tension between documentation, eye-witnessing, and the accusation of manipulation/fictionality repeats itself with regard to the evidence of the second expedition, as well as in the very structure of the novel, which thus plays with the idea of factual documentation versus fake. It's always the same problem: collected specimens as evidence are lost or destroyed on the way back to the home country.[12]

The Amazonian plateau is described as a dreamland, initially in almost Edenic terms. Yet it is a fallen Eden, with threatening snakes. The British explorers participate in the struggle against the pre-historic ape-men, thus helping to ensure the victory and ascendancy of man in the temporal scheme of evolution. These ape-men may be understood as an example for the widespread Edwardian fantasy/fear regarding the so-called "missing link" in the evolutionary chain connecting humans and non-humans. In fact, at the novel's beginning, in a scene where Malone talks to his love interest (who spurs him on to the adventure, as in a medieval quest romance), and reflects on the relation between sex and violence, the novel introduces the theme of a "race memory" that lives underneath the varnish of civilized modern life (Doyle: 4). Most strikingly, Professor Challenger is likened to the king of the ape-men, so that primitive and modern man become mirrors of each other.[13] This superimposition of times, and the "memory of race," are complemented by the personal memory of the narrator who claims he will never forget what he has seen: "Every action of that period will stand out as hard and clear as do the first strange happenings of our childhood. No new impressions could efface those which are so deeply cut" (Doyle: 164). In the final scene of the

---

[12] This was also the case with much of the specimens collected by the Victorian scientists Henry Walter Bates and Alfred Russel Wallace (Glaubrecht: 562).
[13] According to Josephine Sharoni, the novel explores here, as other examples of contemporary literature, the motif of the "double" (Sharoni: 89 ff).

novel, when the flying dinosaur appears in the London lecture hall, the narrator thus links the time of childhood and primeval times: "It was the devil of our childhood in person" (Doyle: 184). Through these scenes the novel acknowledges the role of the imagination that is *impressed* by what it has seen, or has indeed merely imagined.

The Lost World was partly inspired by contemporary discussions of palaeontology. Thus, Arthur Conan Doyle was directly involved with the then notorious case of the so-called Piltdown man, a palaeontological hoax that was only revealed as such in the 1950s, and which consisted in the combination of the jaw of an orangutan and the cranium of a man. This specimen was discovered in the Sussex Downs, where Arthur Conan Doyle was living at the time, when it was widely publicized and discussed at the Geological Society of London. In Sussex also footprints of a fossil iguanodon had been recently discovered, and Doyle included a photographic reproduction of this image in the deluxe edition of the novel (Duncan: x). Yet the novel self-consciously undermines this indexical relation to truth, by pointing out the parallel between faked photographs and faked bones. Moreover, landscape and palaeontological traces ultimately reinforce a parallel between the English plains and the Brazilian plateau, even as the characters wonder whether, while being in the latter, they have "forgotten" the twentieth century.

Therefore, the novel suggests various ways in which the spatial and temporal distance—supposedly marked by the gulf of civilizational progress—might collapse and thus approximate England and the Brazilian wilderness. The South American plateau, Maple White Land, is compared with the prehistoric landscape of Sussex, where the evidence of dinosaurs has left tracks "all over the Hastings sands, in Kent, and in Sussex" (Doyle: 102). Most strikingly, the dishevelled Professor Challenger, apostrophized as the "Columbus of Science," seems not very distinct from an image of primitive man, or indeed the king of the ape-men: "A single day seemed to have changed him from the highest product of modern civilization to the most depraved savage in South America" (Doyle: 144). This uncanny proximity between civilization and its other has shaped the contemporary literature of colonialism and adventure, as in novels by H. G. Wells and Joseph Conrad (Duncan: xi). As the narrator puts it: "There are strange red depths in the soul of the most commonplace man" (Doyle: 145). When the travelers finally reach the plateau, the provisional bridge breaks down, and hence also the possibility of holding the two worlds in a unified vision (Döring):

> We had been natives of the world; now we were natives of the plateau. The two things were separate and apart. There was the plain which led to the canoes. Yonder, beyond the violet, hazy horizon, was the stream which led back to civilization. But the link between was missing. No human ingenuity could suggest a means of bridging the chasm which yawned between ourselves and our past lives. (Doyle: 103)

Even as the novel plays with the continuity of the present with primeval times, the missing "links" suggest not so much the idea of evolution *per se*, but rather that of an atavistic regress, as if to suggest the fragility of modern civilization.

If Verne's novel preserves a Romantic perspective within a clearly progress-oriented scheme, Arthur Conan Doyle's novel confuses the "lost world" and the "new world," so that the disturbing traces of the past maintain a (broken) genealogical connection with the present. Here, the explorers come across a crumpled issue of the newspaper *Chicago Democrat*, material evidence of the earlier American expedition. Modernity itself may become a thing of the past, and during a moment when all hope seems lost, the narrator, Malone, muses on what future explorers, surveying the plateau with a "monoplane," will make out of *their* remains and traces. Not only do the pre-historic animals recall the harpies from Virgil's *Aeneid*, or medieval gargoyles, the flying dinosaurs are also likened to an "aerodrome upon a race day" (Doyle: 86, 104). This superimposition and co-presence of temporalities, I would argue, points to a crisis, a self-doubt of the modern rational spirit and belief in the progress of civilization. This time-specific "darkening of the tropics" (Leys Stepan: 48 ff) marks the historical difference between Verne and Doyle, as well as the different concepts of temporality and knowledge projected onto the cultural and natural "other" of the Amazon region.

References

Primary Sources

Doyle, Arthur Conan. *The Lost World* [1912]. Oxford: Oxford University Press, 2008.

Verne, Jules. *La Jangada. Huit cents lieues sur l'Amazone*. Paris: J. Hetzel, 1881.

Secondary Sources

Conrad, Joseph. *Heart of Darkness* [1899]. London: Penguin, 1983.

Vargas Llosa, Mario. *El sueño del celta*. Madrid: Alfaguara, 2010.

Critical References

Abreu, Márcia. "A Transnational Literate Community: Reactions to Novels in Europe and Brazil." In Márcia Abreu (ed.), *The Transatlantic Circulation of Novels between Europe and Brasil, 1789-1914*. London: Palgrave Macmillan, 2014: 15-38.

Borges, Andrea. "Vamos ao Brasil com Jules Verne? Processos editoriais e civilização nas *Voyages Extraordinaires*." *Revista Sociedade e Estado*, 273 (2012): 494-517.

Deville, Patrick. *Amazonia*. Paris: Éditions du Seuil, 2019.

Döring, Tobias. "Scales and Ladders: Natural History and Map Media in Conan Doyle's *The Lost World* and Wilson Harris' *The Secret Ladder*." In Elmar Schenkel and Stefan Welz (eds.), *Lost Worlds and Mad Elephants. Literature, Science and Technology 1700-1900*. Glienicke and Cambridge, Mass.: Galda and Wilch, 1999: 243-258.

Duncan, Ian. "Introduction." In Arthur Conan Doyle, *The Lost World* [1912]. Oxford: Oxford University Press, 2008.

Dünne, Jörg. *Die katastophische Feerie. Geschichte, Geologie und Spektakel in der modernen französischen Literatur*. Konstanz: Konstanz University Press, 2016.

Fabian, Johannes. *Time and the Other: How Anthropology Makes its Object*. New York: Columbia University Press, 2002.

Ginzburg, Carlo. "Clues: Roots of an Evidential Paradigm." In *Clues, Myths, and the Historical Method*, transl. John and Anne C. Tedeschi. Baltimore: Johns Hopkins, 1989: 87-113.

Glaubrecht, Matthias."Am Anfang war der Amazonas. Die Entdeckung Brasiliens und des 'Flusses der Amazonen,'" Postface. In Alfred Russel Wallace, *Abenteuer am Rio Amazonas und am Rio Negro* [*A Narrative of Travels on the Amazon and Rio Negro*, 1853], transl. Anonymous and Michael Schickenberg. Berlin: Galiani, 2014: 523-583.

González Echevarría, Roberto. "A Lost World Rediscovered: Sarmiento's *Facundo*." In T. Halperin Donghi *et alii* (eds.), *Sarmiento. Author of a Nation*. Berkeley: University of California Press, 1994: 220-256.

Henrikson, Paula and Christina Kullberg. *Time and Temporalities in European Travel Writing*. London: Routledge, 2021.

Leys Stepan, Nancy. *Picturing Tropical Nature*. London: Reaktion Books, 2001.

Pizarro, Ana. *Amazônia. As vozes do Rio*. Belo Horizonte: Editora UFMG, 2012.

Rogers, Charlotte. *Mourning El Dorado. Literature and Extractivism in the Contemporary American Tropics*. Charlottesville and London: University of Virginia Press, 2019.

Sharoni, Josephine. *Lacan and Fantasy Literature. Portents of Modernity in Late-Victorian and Edwardian Fiction*. Boston and Leiden: Rodopi, 2017.

Siskind, Mariano. *Cosmopolitan Desires. Global Modernity and World Literature in Latin America*. Evanston, Ill.: Northwestern University Press, 2014.

Souza, Márcio. *História da Amazônia. Do período pré-clombiano aos desafios do século XXI*. Rio de Janeiro: Record, 2019.

Stiegler, Bernd. *Spuren, Elfen und andere Erscheinungen. Conan Doyle und die Photographie*. Frankfurt am Main: Fischer, 2014.

Uriarte, Javier. "'Splendid testemunhos.' Documenting Atrocities, Bodies, and Desire in Roger Casement's *Black Diaries*." In *Intimate Frontiers. A Literary Geography of the Amazon*. Liverpool: Liverpool University Press, 2019: 88-112.

Welge, Jobst. "The Jungle Novel. International Permutations of a Genre." In Miriam Lay Brander (ed.), *Genre and Globalization. Transformación de géneros en contextos (post-)coloniales / Transformations des genres dans des contextes (post-)coloniaux*. Hildesheim: Olms, 2017: 207-229.

Wolfzettel, Friedrich. *Jules Verne. Eine Einführung*. München: Artemis & Winkler, 1991.

The Blind Leading the Blind: Brueghel in Ekphrastic Poetry

Orsolya Milián

Works by the soi-disant "Peasant Brueghel" or works attributed to him — such as the *The Parable of the Blind, Landscape with the Fall of Icarus* or *The Hunters in the Snow* — constitute tremendously popular themes in ekphrastic literature, and perhaps the endless polysemy of Brueghel's paintings is one of the principal reasons for the fact that dozens of literary and other media products have remediated his paintings to the present time.[1] Choosing only from the field of literature and from texts relating to Brueghel's *The Parable of the Blind*, besides the two poems examined in the following — that is the American modernist poet and writer William Carlos Williams's *The Parable of the Blind* (1962) and Gisbert Kranz's *Der Blindensturz* (1981)[2]–, one could also scrutinize *Die Blinden* by Josef Weinheber (1937), *Brueghel: Die Parabel von den Blinden* by Erich Lotz (1956), *Die Blinden* by Walter Bauer (1972), *Les Aveugles* by Charles Baudelaire (1868) and the Hungarian modernist poet Mihály Babits's poem entitled *Vakok a hídon* [Blinds on the Bridge] (1913) or Gert Hofmann's novel entitled *Der Blindensturz* (1985).

Williams's *The Parable of the Blind* appeared for the first time in the Spring issue of *The Hudson Review* in 1960, being published in revised form in his 1962 volume entitled *Pictures from Brueghel and*

---

[1] An extended version of this paper has been published in *Primerjalna književnost* 42:2 (2019). 15-34. URL: https://ojs.zrc-sazu.si/primerjalna_knjizevnost/article/view/7476.

[2] The poem was published under the title *Brueghels Blinde* in Kranz's volume of poetry entitled *Niederwald und andere Gedichte* in 1984. But Kranz had already published the poem without any title in an eminent handbook entitled *Das Bildgedicht. Theorie, Lexikon, Bibliographie*, edited by him (Vol. I. Köln-Wien: Böhlau Verlag, 1981. 31). Later on the poem appeared in several anthologies and periodicals: for instance, it was republished in a thematic issue on concrete poetry in the journal entitled *Deutsch Betrifft Uns* in 1986. Kranz also published the poem under the pseudonym Carlo Carduna. Siglind Bruhn published the poem in English in her monograph entitled *Musical Ekphrasis*: 59.

Other Poems, which opened with the title cycle of ten poems (*Pictures from Brueghel*). *The Parable of the Blind* became the ninth part of that cycle of poems. Williams's correspondence reveals that he was considering including reproductions of Brueghel's paintings in his poetry volume, but ultimately abandoned this plan. However, the poem titles — such as *Children's Games, The Hunters in the Snow, Landscape with the Fall of Icarus, The Parable of the Blind* and so on — obviously denominate paintings by or attributed to Brueghel, just as Kranz's poem title *Der Blindensturz* does. In addition, the title of Williams's cycle of poems and several of the poems specify the painter's name. See for example the following excerpts: "Brueghel the painter / concerned with it all" (*The Hunters in the Snow*); "Brueghel saw it all / and with his grim / humor faithfully / recorded / it" (*Children's Games*). The alternate title of Gisbert Kranz's poem (*Brueghels Blinde*) acts exactly in this manner, but beyond that (as it will be shown later on) the poem's typographic configuration also alludes to Brueghel's painting. Hence it is not particularly hard to diagnose the interart connection between the two poems and Brueghel's painting — at any rate, if we are familiar with the painter's body of work.

[Pieter Brueghel the Elder: *The Parable of the Blind* (*The Blind Leading the Blind*). 1568. Museo e Gallerie Nazionale di Capodimonte, Naples]

Brueghel's intentionally polysemous art probably accounts for the fact that although art historians unanimously consider *The Parable of the Blind* a pictorial masterpiece and the painting has engendered many thoughtful explanations, we do not yet have a single, consensually accepted art historical interpretation of it. In essence, interpretations of the painting vary according to whether the onlooker judges it to be a genre painting or an allegorical painting. In the former case the picture would focus closely on human figures engaged in everyday activities: "Brueghel's work depicts the tumbling down of half a dozen blind men holding to each other […]. [T]he crippled, blind beggars and pilgrims, who inseparably belonged to the cityscapes of the time, were primarily understood as comic figures" (Kukla).[3] In Brueghel's time, blindness was also customarily associated with criminality, as it was often a penalty imposed for committing unlawful acts. Blindness was moreover associated with moral corruption, as it was believed to be God's punishment for sin. Since in general blind people could not find any job, they frequently had to fall back on begging.

But it is much more common to decipher Brueghel's *The Parable of the Blind* as an allegorical work founded upon certain texts of Scripture: "Leave them [the Pharisees] alone. They are blind guides! But if a blind person leads another blind person, they will both fall into a ditch" (Matthew 15:14). For instance, Hans Sedlmayr, who devised his famous *Strukturanalyse* (structure analysis) method as applied to Brueghel's *The Parable of the Blind*, sets forth the following probable meanings:

> the painting provides a grim and dreadful atmosphere because of the parabolic arc proceeding downwards and the use of some alarming colors in the lower part of the picture, while one of the horizontals in the upper part of it expresses calmness through the completely amiable quality of coloring. The original, literal meaning refers to the conception of blinds as empty-headed people prevailing in the late 16th century, while the allegorical meanings evoke the idea of 'the blind leading the blind' that is the parable of the world turned upside down and blind people symbolizing zealous, errant souls. An additional eschatological meaning brings forth the

---

[3] All translations are mine unless otherwise specified.

inexorability of the fall and touches on the last things of human destiny (such as death), thus it assigns the additional meaning of fatelessness to the tranquil landscape, the location of the plot. Finally, Brueghel's painting possesses a tropological meaning, too, inasmuch as it encourages the viewers to classify their own selves as belonging among the zealous, errant souls and interpret the representation as a call for (better) self-comprehension. (Sedlmayr, quoted in Imdahl: 90)

Accordingly, Brueghel's representation of blindness may refer to sin, a stroke of fate, bigotry or an aberration from a religious system of beliefs, but it might also mean untrainedness or a lack of intellect or self-understanding.

It is worth mentioning that the village church in the background of the painting is noticeably similar to St. Anna Pede at the village of Dilbeek (Belgium), which still stands today. Brueghel's painting may had been inspired by or might illustrate the parable of Jesus, but it might also be based on a common maxim, the widely known Flemish saying of "the blind leading the blind," especially considering that Brueghel himself had often created drawings and paintings on the subject of proverbs, most notably in works such as *Big Fish Eat Little Fish* (1556), *Twelve Proverbs* (1558) and *Netherlandish Proverbs* (1559). The last one features a small trio of blind men, a line of beggars in the background, thus it is a specific visual representation of the well-known proverb and a prefiguration of *The Parable of the Blind*. Be that as it may, this painting shows Brueghel's ability to create mesmerizing allegorical works based either on religious doctrines or popular proverbs.

Like the sightless beggars in the foreground, the church in the background also called forth various, conflicting interpretations. According to some scholars, the building does not bear any iconographic meaning at all, being merely a typical element of Flemish countryside (Hagen and Hagen: 193), while others suggest it is a religious symbol which brings to the forefront the parabolic and moralistic discourse of Brueghel's painting. As its vertical axis splits the group of people heading towards their inevitable fate into two, dividing those who are already falling from those who are just wavering as yet, it might indicate that while the first two men in the line of beggars are already beyond recovery, those at the end of the row might let go of one another and avoid falling into the swamp — thus, they still might be saved. One of Brueghel's most brilliant ideas was to cut the church spire off the upper edge of the picture with the frame. As a consequence, it is impossible to decide whether we are looking at a Catholic or a Reformed church and whether, to use Sedlmayr's terms, the "zealous, errant souls" of the blind people interpreted along the lines of Matthew's Gospel belong to one denomination or the other. In other words, we cannot tell, from the pictorial syntax alone, whether this painting, which was created during the period of religious wars waged in the 16th century, signifies an anti-Catholic or an anti-Protestant or anti-sect[4] representation or whether — as Sedlmayr has argued — its meanings have to be constructed on a more universal level.

Williams's and Kranz's poems both offer descriptions of Brueghel's *The Parable of the Blind* and both of them are ekphrases, but even a brief look reveals some striking dissimilarities, especially the fact that the typographical or visuospatial arrangement of Kranz's poem forms a configuration, an image with potential meanings, while Williams's poem uses a more traditional page-setting. Williams demediates or dematerializes Brueghel's painting, but at the same time preserves verbal traces of the pictorial medium that was effaced and erased from the material level of poetic signification. Phrasings like "without a red" (which draws our attention to the absence of vivid colors from Brueghel's painting), the words "the canvas" and "the composition"-the latter occurring three times — or allusions to the process of viewing (such as "a peasant / cottage *is seen*," emphasis mine) and the agency or

---

[4] By the time Brueghel painted *The Parable of the Blind* in 1568, many religious sects had appeared in the Low Countries, such as the Lutherans, the Zwinglians, the Frankists (followers of Sebastian Frank), the Spiritualists and the Servetiens, as well as the Anabaptists. As Margaret A. Sullivan argues along the lines of the Gospel of Matthew: "The charge of blindness could be applied to the church — the priests who kept concubines and the convents and abbeys that failed to carry out their mission of caring for lepers and the needy, as well as the multiple sects who put their own understanding of the Bible above the wisdom of the church fathers — but for Bruegel's viewers the number of blind men in the painting made the sects, each with its own dogma and interpretation of the Bible, the most obvious candidates for criticism."

functioning of the painting (such as "the composition shows"; "no seeing man / is represented") might be considered as traces or marks of the pictorial that had been imprinted on the verbal medium. Williams's poem begins with an appreciative but ambivalent praise ("this horrible but superb painting"), before describing and narrating the painting in a laconic manner, typical of Williams. At the same time or perhaps even more importantly, the poem also provides a narrative of the activity and process of viewing — in the words of James Heffernan "a narrative of the viewer's eye in motion" (Heffernan: 168) — as if we were to follow the wandering eye of the lyrical subject, which itself seems to look for the correlations among the particular visual details. Instead of comprehensively itemizing the observed objects and the spatial, syntactic or semantic relations among them, Williams's *The Parable of the Blind* emphasizes the process or the event of visual perception, and because of that it seems that the most prolific interpretation of Williams's poem would consist in analyzing how the speaking subject views, rather than what he views.

It is quite striking that when the viewer (and the mediator of the painting) enumerates details of the painting, he provides minimal information about the spatial layout of the visual components. In this fashion, the diagonally downward line of human figures clinging to each other is described in detail — in proportion to Williams's laconicism — e.g. "leading / each other diagonally downward"; "one / follows the others stick in / hand"), while no information is disclosed about the precise location of the elements of the rural scenery (such as "the peasant cottage" or the "church spire"), and these are mentioned only briefly, as if incidentally. This particular viewer of the painting seems to be mainly interested in the human figures, the blind beggars and the catastrophe, the downfall to which their marching ultimately leads, and which can only be witnessed by the painting's actual viewer, since "no seeing man / is represented" on Brueghel's painting. (As I shall point out later on, this does not necessarily mean that Williams's poem would only recognize the significance of Brueghel's painting in the representation of blind people left to themselves by the able-bodied community, and as a result interpreting it as genre painting only.)

The threefold occurrence of "composition" might be read as a reference to the structuredness and the visual code of the painting, but we can also correlate it—especially the lines of "there is no detail extraneous / to the composition"—with the composition of the poem itself. Accordingly, this self-reflexive remark may draw our attention to the fact that though the painting is not re*presen*ted by the poem in the spatial or literal sense, Williams's poem itself has an organized, structured and meaningful form, and as such by reason of the artistic shaping of its verbal signs is equal or at least related to the respective painting. As A. D. Baker has argued in his doctoral thesis in connection with Williams's cycle of poems *Pictures from Brueghel*: "The method of the poems is deceptively simple: they appear to be casual restatements of an original picture, but a discrete art in their organization makes them verbal artifacts in their own right" (Baker: 162). We might perceive this gesture as a declarative self-description that effaces the picture from the poem's discourse by hinting at its own linguistic capacities, the power of verbal "composition" or the force of the poem's taciturn character and its success; at the minimum, it brings itself and the linguistic aspect into prominence. Therefore, this motif of rivalry would prove that the poem is able to "catch up with" or be an equal to the painting and it might even exceed it in its effect on the recipient or the powerful representation of the dreadful threat of downfall.

Williams significantly rearranged the lines of *The Parable of the Blind* for the volume edition, especially with regard to the last four stanzas, so presumably he was preoccupied with the physical layout of his poem on a book page, that is to say, apparently, he was interested in his text's visuality. Despite that, the final form of the poem does not display the pursuit of configuring words into an optical image; the redesigned page-setting makes no attempt to fit in the emblematic or pattern poetry traditions. The visuospatial presentation of this *vers libre* poem and the use of enjambments make the poem's sonority, its phonesthesia and aural rhythm, a priority. Williams, who was an amateur painter as well, alludes to the visual dimension only by resorting to words that can be read aloud. The lineation of *The Parable of the Blind* fundamentally serves the smooth continuity of the lyrical voice's flow (and its readability in such a way) and does not endeavor to arrest or freeze its movement into a visual shape or spatialize it through the typographical placement of words.

At first glance it may seem that the reverse process is taking place in Kranz's poem: this text is incontrovertibly held together by a visual pattern, these lines of poetry are made to fit a visual shape as well, and their meanings can be accessed through the process of deciphering both the words and the visuospatiality of the textual fragments arranged on the white book page. (Not to mention the fact that if we do not speak German at all, we might either see the poem as a meaningless visual form or — if we recognize the remediation of Brueghel's painting as displayed here — comprehend it as a visually *meaningful* pattern only.) Naturally, the optical image here becomes apparent only through the (re)mediation of writing and the typographical arrangement of the text, and as a consequence we cannot state that Kranz's poem entirely frees the visual from the domineering ambitions of language. Nonetheless, while trying to construe the text/image suture of *Der Blindensturz* we must constantly make decisions about whether we read or view the poem, since in this mixed media format (as well as in calligrams or pattern poems in general) the image and the text cannot be perceived at the same time; nor can they both be understood at the same time. Thus, one might tentatively argue that in its semiotic war between texts and images, the image-text dialectic of Kranz's poem stages an encounter of equals. Or at least it sets ups a duel between *more equal* participants, especially as compared with the bulk of the ekphrastic literary tradition, which tends to subordinate the visual to the textual/verbal.

As might be seen from the above, I would steer clear of identifying the word-and-image relation in Kranz's poem as a peaceful coexistence. Perhaps it is sufficient to refer to those fruitful tensions that arise from reading and/or looking at the block of text in the upper right corner of the poem:

>   l
>   i
>   n
>   ks
>   liegen
>   lässt die kirche[5]

One could decode this layout of words as an image of a towered church or a church with a steeple, but in no way would it be interpreted as such by all readers/viewers. Moreover, it is open to debate whether this connotation has built on the knowledge that Kranz's poem remediates Brueghel's painting or whether it has been formulated owing to the fact that the word "kirche" [*church*] features in the fragment. In the former case a recollection of an example of fine art or a visual remnant is driving the interpretation, while in the latter case a verbal element is influencing or even guiding the process of construction of meanings. If one identifies this excerpt as a visual tautology of the word "kirche" [*church*] and one's understanding is driven primarily or solely by that solitary word (or the verbal medium itself), the visual form or pattern will actually be endowed with the function of an illustration, an appendix or supplement that complements the text. In this case the image becomes subordinated to the word.

Resembling to some extent Williams's poem, Kranz's ekphrastic calligram or calligrammatic ekphrasis denotes the downward direction of the blind people's route as well as their fate, the "disaster." But here the typographic arrangement of the block of text in the lower left corner of the book page itself shows a gradual, diagonal and downward movement that can be conceived as such both through the visual perception of the fragment and the Western convention of reading from left to right:

---

[5] "ignoring the church to the left […]," trans. Bruhn: 59.

> augenlos, der sich
>   hält am stab von
>   augenlos, der sich
>   hält am leib von
>   augenlos, der sich
>   hält am leib von
>   augenlos, der sich
>   hält am stab von
>   augenlos, der sich
>   hält am leib von
>   augenlos, der
>   stürzt
>   bo-
>   den-
>   los[6]

In addition, the vertical layout of the words ending the poem ("der stürzt bodenlos" [*who falls bottomless*]) conjures up in itself the notion of falling, while the lack of punctuation at the ending of *Der Blindensturz* indicates the continuous or infinite nature of the fall. Nevertheless, in order to interpret the downward line as the route of blind people connected to each other, one must inevitably rely on language, the repetition of the word "augenlos" ("eyeless" or "blind") and the verbal description of their march. While Williams's poem does not localize the "church" (in Williams's words "the church spire") within the literary space of the ekphrasis, not only do the two parts of Kranz's poem that are visually and typographically separated from each other mirror the arrangement of the main syntactical elements of Brueghel's painting, but the empty space between the two blocks of text r*epresents* the spatial distance between the chief compositional constituents of the painting, and — if we take verbal meanings into account as well — the physical-spatial or religious distance between the blind people and the church.

Kranz's *Der Blindensturz* seems to give a more substantial role to the "church" than Williams's *The Parable of the Blind*, and it looks as though this increased significance is primarily assignable to the

---

[6] "eyeless, who holds on the staff of eyeless, who holds on to the body of eyeless, who holds on to the body of eyeless, who holds on the staff of eyeless, who holds on to the body of eyeless, who falls bottomless." Transl. Bruhn: 59.

visuospatial arrangement of its blocks of text and the visual shape of the excerpt incorporating the word "kirche." As mentioned earlier, Williams's ekphrasis seems to relegate the church to an ancillary role and place much more emphasis on the fate of the blind men, while Kranz's ekphrastic pattern poem elevates the church to a protagonist—not only verbally, but visually, too. These procedures of remediation may show that the two poems have conflicting preferences concerning the distinctly different interpretive traditions of Brueghel's work. In this respect one could state that Williams's poem is prone to comprehend Brueghel's *The Parable of the Blind* as a genre painting, while Kranz's poem tends towards grasping it as an allegorical depiction; however, their impact on the interpretive possibilities of the misfortune or the disaster mentioned in the poems' endings seems to be worthy of closer scrutiny.

Discussing Kranz's *Der Blindensturz*, Siglind Bruhn notes that "the German expression 'links liegen lassen' is particularly powerful, since it covers both the literal observation that the blind men pass the church, 'leaving it behind to their left,' and the figurative meaning of 'deliberately not taking notice of it'" (Bruhn: 60). While in the literal sense the words just signify walking past a building, in the metaphorical sense both translational choices mark a turning away from "the church" (that is falling away from God and one or all of the religious sects) or a practice of false religion; moreover, the latter solution ("deliberately not taking notice of it") implies that the blind men's way of acting rests on an intentional and conscious decision. If we favor metaphorical implications and take them into consideration together with the relationship of the two visuospatially separate blocks of text of the poem, *Der Blindensturz* will establish the quality of the attitude towards "the church"–that is the turning away from it—as the chief reason and explanation for the blind people's "bottomless fall." It can be readily accepted that the interpretations of this complex state of affairs may vary vastly; however, the multiplication and dissemination of meanings depend on how one decodes "the church." For example, besides the literal and figurative meaning of "stumbling" the word "fall" may also denote that the human characters will be doomed to Hell for eternity. (And who exactly will be condemned to Hell? The Catholic errant or the Protestant?)

At first glance, Williams's poem seems to omit completely the allegorical aspects of Brueghel's painting. It is almost as though an amateur or a dilettante spectator was viewing Brueghel's *The Parable of the Blind*, reaching the conclusion that the "beggars" will "stumble finally into a bog" and that it will cause their "disaster" (that is, they will lose their way in the morass and may even drown there). This ekphrasis does not attribute central importance to the "church," but even so, the weight of the word "disaster," which concludes the poem, retunes the strayed blind men's stumbling into the swamp. The ending of the poem hardly touches upon eternal punishment or everlasting damnation, but it brings an aggregate tragedy, the wanderers' stumbling to death and the risks of zealotry (e.g. following a leader blindly), to the fore all the more.

Far from being merely faithful descriptions, literary ekphrases produce interpretive commentaries on their visual objects, usually exploiting the polysemic potential of pictures in order to employ, reinforce or erode their commonly accepted (or contested) meanings. Insofar as they offer diverse handlings and interpretations of their subject matter, ekphrases perform a hermeneutical function, brushing up, expanding and/or modifying our cultural body of knowledge of visual or mixed media works of art. Viewed in this light, Kranz's poem seems to utilize the arguably more generally accepted (i. e. religious) meanings attributed to Brueghel's painting, while Williams's poem, relying upon the interpretations of Brueghel's work of art as a genre painting – and perhaps on the meaning of the proverb, too –, highlights the "everyday" perils of poor leadership that leads its followers to their demise.

Ekphrases are never just verbal refigurations or translations of a pre-existing visual work of art, but they themselves create and shape what becomes worded at all. While Williams's poem effaces the visual (Brueghel's painting) keeping its traits in verbal allusions only and in a sense repressing the image in order to create its own verbal "self-portrait," Kranz's poem adds another filter or stratum to the mediatization of Brueghel's painting through verbal description, namely the typographic image of the verbal text which exhibits the "skeleton" of the original pictorial composition as well. As opposed to Williams's more conventional ekphrasis, Kranz' also rearranges the traditional word-image hierarchy of ekphrases (that tend to give supremacy to words) in that the poem vindicates a more "democratic" or balanced relation between the verbal and the visual medium. In this way Kranz's poem urges us to take a reflexive look at the mediation of pictures and texts and the relationships between them in a more forceful and vigorous manner.

References

Primary sources

William Carlos Williams, *Pictures from Brueghel and Other Poems*. New York: New Directions, 1962.

Gisbert Kranz. *Der Blindensturz*. In Siglind Bruhn, *Musical Ekphrasis. Composers Responding to Poetry and Painting*. Hillsdale, New York: Pendragon Press, 2000.

Critical references

Baker, A. D. "The Act of Seeing: Poem, Image and the Work of William Carlos Williams." Doctoral Thesis, 1982. Durham University. Durham E-Theses Online (etheses.dur.ac.uk). Web. 29 Dec. 2019. URL: http://etheses.dur.ac.uk/7815/

Hagen, Rose-Marie and Rainer Hagen. *What Great Paintings Say*. Vol. 2, Köln: Taschen, 2003.

Imdahl, Max. *Giotto. Arénafreskók*, transl. Kerekes Amália. Budapest: Kijárat Kiadó, 2003.

Heffernan, James A. W. *Museum of Words. The Poetics of Ekphrasis from Homer to Ashbery*. Chicago and London: University of Chicago Press, 1993.

Kukla, Krisztián. "Okuláris okulás. (Id. Pieter Bruegel *Vakok* című festményének interpretációi)." Web. 29 Dec. 2019. URL: http://www.c3.hu/~gond/tartalom/18-19/frakukla.html

Sullivan, Margaret A. "Peasant and Nestrobber: Bruegel as Witness of His Times." *Journal of Historians of Netherlandish Art*, 7.2 (2015): Web. 29 Dec. 2019. URL: https://jhna.org/articles/peasant-nestrobber-bruegel-witness-of-his-times/

ibidem.eu